I0140386

Rebuilding Zion

An Exposition of the Books of the Exile

F B Hole

Scripture Truth Publications

The Lost Diadem first published in *Scripture Truth* Volume 4 (1912) and in revised form in Volume 40 (1959-1961).

Daniel, Ezra, Nehemiah, Haggai, Zechariah and *Malachi* first published in *Scripture Truth* Volume 40 (1959-1961).

First edition ©1972 Central Bible Hammond Trust, London.

Transferred to Digital Printing 2021

Revised edition (re-typeset, with minor amendments) © 2021 Scripture Truth Publications

ISBN: 978-0-901860-71-2 (paperback)

A publication of Scripture Truth

All rights reserved. No part of this publication may be reproduced, stored in a retrieval system, or transmitted, in any form or by any means, electronic, mechanical, photocopying, recording or otherwise without prior permission of Scripture Truth Publications.

Scripture quotations, unless otherwise indicated, are taken from The Authorized (King James) Version. Rights in the Authorized Version are vested in the Crown. Reproduced by permission of the Crown's patentee, Cambridge University Press.

Scripture quotations marked (New Trans.) are taken from "The Holy Scriptures, a New Translation from the Original Languages" by J. N. Darby (G Morrish, 1890).

Cover photograph ©iStockphoto.com/alexsl (Alex Slobodkin)

Published by Scripture Truth Publications
31-33 Glover Street, Crewe, Cheshire, CW1 3LD

Scripture Truth is an imprint of Central Bible Hammond Trust, a charitable trust

Typesetting by John Rice

CONTENTS

REBUILDING ZION

Foreword

Frank Binford Hole's contribution to the supply of sound Christian literature is immense. Whether contributing articles to his own publication *Edification* or *Scripture Truth*, which he edited from 1943 to 1962, his explanations of Scripture are lucid and constructive, with an eye always on the practical implications for contemporary Christians.

This collection of Bible studies on the Old Testament books covering the period of Israel's exile from their homeland, and their subsequent return, is an inspiring account of how their prophetic message, far from only having relevance to a situation distant in time and place, still speaks with energetic force to us today.

First published in book form in 1972 but out of print for several years, it has been a joy to prepare this edition for publication. The text has been checked against the original articles in *Scripture Truth*. As usual, Scripture references have been corrected as necessary, and a few sentences with no bearing on the author's exposition have been omitted. Re-reading the text several times in the course of preparation, I never cease to be grateful to the author for the clear manner in which he explains often complex prophecies in a way which emphasises their vital message for Christians today.

When the book was first published in 1972, the introductory chapter "The Lost Diadem" was included in its second version, from the late 1950s. Somehow the original article from 1912 seems more appropriate today, so I have included this by way of an introduction, but for completeness have retained the second version in an appendix.

It is my prayer that as you read, the Holy Spirit will help you understand how these prophets, writing under His direction, had a message not only for their own generations but for ours too.

John Rice

April 2021

The Lost Diadem[1]

To say that the outstanding feature of the present age is the wellnigh universal spirit of unrest is to utter merely a platitude. The thing is so obtrusive as to be patent to even the most frivolous mind.

Unrest, upheaval, clashing of interests, conflict, these are no new things in the earth. When, since the far-off days of peaceful Eden in innocence, did they *not* exist? Never a year since the blight and curse of sin descended on this world but they have been painfully manifest.

Admitting this, however, we venture to affirm that the present epidemic of unrest and upheaval has already assumed such proportions that it may justly be termed the feature of the age; and further, with the Bible as guide, to predict that it will yet increase until the stiff gale becomes a perfect hurricane.

The unrest existing today has about it two features which are worthy of notice:

1. *It is practically universal in its extent.* Every country of note is afflicted with it. The civilization may be Eastern and ancient as in China, or Western and modern as in

[1] *Scripture Truth*, Volume 4, 1912, page 147

Britain and America; it matters not, upheaval is threatened, and who shall say the force and fury of the eruption when it comes?

2. *The unrest today is touching every department of human thought and activity.* It never did this before. Many an empire has risen and flourished and decayed, whilst repose has rested upon the world of philosophy or of the applied sciences. Today violent changes are marked in all directions. Men's minds are working with almost superhuman energy in the manufacture of new ideas and theories: social, political, and theological.

What does it all mean? That is the question which surely must be uppermost in the mind of every sober observer. For the Christian who bows to the Word of God and accepts its sayings there is no difficulty in discovering the divinely given answers. Human histories give us at the best imperfect details of a few of the most tragic happenings of time; the Bible alone puts into our hands the golden thread of divine purpose running through all history. Let us attempt humbly to seize the divine thought by the guidance of the Holy Spirit of God that we may obtain the divine answer.

*   *   *   *

Most of our readers are aware of the fact that before the Flood government did not exist. That age culminated in such violent corruption and unrest that destruction was God's only remedy (see Genesis 6:1-13).

On the cleansed earth government was instituted in the person of Noah (Genesis 9:1-6). After the break-up of Babel the authority seems to have departed from the main line of Noah's descendants, and each separate family began to range itself under its own tribal head, and the idea of kingship arose. There was no fresh development in regard to government on God's part until He called His people Israel out of Egypt, that *He*, the great JEHOVAH, might exercise authority in their midst. The moment He chose for doing this was most significant. Egypt, almost the oldest of the nations, had just risen to the highest point of her glory, having expelled the alien dynasties of 'shepherd kings', and being united under the rule of powerful and warlike Pharaohs who carried their conquests to the Euphrates. Then it was that God asserted His right to His people, and smote the proud oppressor a heavy blow which evidently marked the beginning of decline for that empire. He carried His people, though much hindered by their perverseness, into the land of promise. Jehovah claimed that land as His, taking possession of it by His people. He claimed it as His in token that the whole earth is His. Twice is He spoken of as 'Lord of all the earth' in connection with the passage of the Jordan (Joshua 3:11, 13).

Arrived in the land of promise, the people soon tired of being peculiar in having God alone as their leader, and clamoured for a king (1 Samuel 8). This, though a serious departure from God, was permitted and, after they had had bitter experience of the man after their own hearts, God raised up the man after His own heart and delegated to him His visible authority in the world, placing him as a shepherd over His people and extending his kingdom by crowning his arms with success. The diadem—which was properly the diadem, not of Israel only, but of the whole world—was placed upon his brow and confirmed to his seed. For a brief moment it was worn by him and Solomon his successor.

Then the inevitable story of decline. The kingdom divided; the smaller half only following the wearers of David's diadem, and they growing less and less powerful as the departure, in spite of occasional revivals God-given, became more and more pronounced.

At last the end came. Zedekiah, the last wearer of the diadem—though perhaps he wore it only in name—added treachery to his sins and dishonoured the name of his God, whereupon, as recorded no less than *three* times in Scripture (2 Kings 25; 2 Chronicles 36; Jeremiah 52), Jerusalem fell before the Babylonians, and the dominion passed into the hands of Nebuchadnezzar, 'the times of the Gentiles' setting in.

It was just at this time that by the pen of Ezekiel a prophecy was given. As the diadem—which was, be it remembered, that not only of Israel, but of the whole earth—fell from the brow of the last apostate prince of David's line, struck thence by the hand of God in retributive judgment, these words were written. They are so important that we venture to quote them in full.

'And thou, profane wicked prince of Israel, whose day is come, when iniquity shall have an end, Thus saith the Lord GOD: Remove the diadem, and take off the crown: this shall not be the same: exalt him that is low, and abase him that is high. I will overturn, overturn, overturn, it: and it shall be no more, until He come whose right it is; and I will give it Him' (Ezekiel 21:25-27).

*   *   *   *

How wonderfully illuminating! How steady the beam of light here thrown over the dark pages of human history since that day! The diadem has indeed been removed, and if a comprehensive history of the world were compiled it would prove to be but a record of the various efforts of men and nations to exalt themselves and seize upon the diadem, and of the sure and skilful way in which, just as they appeared certain of success, God has abased and overturned them.

A vision of this was granted to the prophet Daniel (chapter 7). It confirmed the dream previously given to Nebuchadnezzar (chapter 2). For a brief moment it seemed as if the diadem was to belong to that great king. But exalting himself he was painfully abased in abject madness, and soon his great Babylon fell and was overturned. So too with the succeeding empires— Persian, Greek, and Roman. Each ran their day and each was overturned at the end.

Since the dissolution of the Roman Empire no great empire, holding practically the civilized earth in its grip, has been permitted to arise. Today Europe resembles an armed camp. The diadem of the earth is lost; it is 'no more'. No one nation dare attempt to regain it. The very effort, they know, would be their overturning.

The present state of extremely unstable equilibrium cannot, however, go on for ever. Political leaders feel this and talk vaguely of the coming 'Armageddon', meaning thereby a great conflict which will embroil practically all the civilized earth. They appear to forget that the real Armageddon is not a frightful conflict of man against man, but rather a cruel and impious hurling of the united forces of men against God (see Revelation 16:13-16).

It is more than possible, however, that these vague warnings of coming ills uttered by human leaders do herald the near approach of the true Armageddon! Their words, like those of Caiaphas in John 11:49-52, may mean more than they themselves are conscious of. New forces of great strength have arisen in these later years. They centre themselves round the idea of 'the brotherhood of man' based on 'the universal fatherhood of God'. Socialism, Unitarianism, the new, progressive, humanistic theology, are all branches of this root idea. Their use in the hands of Satan is to prepare the way for the last great federation of mankind, to get ready for Antichrist.

It might be objected by some that the Messiah to whom the diadem belonged by right has already come. He has indeed, but He came not asserting those rights, but allowing man to have his hour and the power of darkness to assert itself that He might accomplish redemption. Satan, who profanely has usurped the diadem, actually offered it to Him in the temptation in the wilderness. He refused it, and chose not that short and easy cut to glory, but the toilsome road that led through death and resurrection— 'ought not Christ to have suffered these things, and to enter into His glory?' (Luke 24:26).

He did, however, plainly predict the coming of another prince who would accept a diadem—purporting to be the true diadem of the earth—from the hands of Satan. 'I am come in My Father's name, and ye receive Me not: if another shall come in his own name, him ye will receive' (John 5:43).

In the days of the coming great trinity of evil—the dragon, the beast, and the false prophet, spoken of in Revelation 13—it will seem as if at last Ezekiel's prophecy was reversed and nullified. Mankind already shows symptoms of going 'federation-mad'. It will then have federated itself into such a condition of so-called 'brotherhood' that it will only need the appearance of an unscrupulous 'superman', energized by Satan, for him to seize the reins of power and institute the most monstrous tyranny the world will ever witness. Let that state of things be reached, and what can save men from the net they have cast for their own feet? It is quite possible that many, even a vast majority, may support and glory in the tyranny established. They will say, 'Peace and safety', thinking that at last the diadem is recovered so permanently that no more overturnings need be feared.

'When they shall say, Peace and safety; then sudden destruction cometh upon them' (1 Thessalonians 5:3). The last line of Ezekiel's prophecy will find sudden fulfilment. The last great overturning will take place in the true Armageddon, when both beast and false prophet and their armies are destroyed by the sudden appearing of Him 'whose right it is'.

In that day the long-lost diadem, brilliant then, not only with the gems of creation, but the brighter jewels of redemption, will be brought forth and placed upon the head of the once rejected Man of Nazareth, our adorable Lord Jesus. Upon His sacred brow the diadem will have found its permanent, its eternal resting-place.

*   *   *   *

In view of these things, dear brethren in Christ, let us not be disturbed in mind. Let us be only concerned that we keep flying the flag of true testimony to Christ. Let us not join hands with the world, nor aid its schemes and movements which are paving the way for Antichrist. Let us abide in communion with the Father and the Son, and treasure in our hearts the thought that all the unrest and the overturning is only 'UNTIL HE

COME'. Shall we not turn our eyes toward the sun-rising of that day, saying, 'Even so, come, Lord Jesus'?

Daniel

INTRODUCTION

Isaiah prophesied in Judah both before and also during the reign of the God-fearing Hezekiah, when under his influence things seemed outwardly to be better. Yet the prophet had to reveal the hidden corruption under the surface. In our Bibles his book is followed by that of Jeremiah, who was raised up of God to speak for Him in the last sad days of Judah's history, when things were hopelessly bad and beyond recovery, and the blow fell on them through Nebuchadnezzar.

The seven nations of Canaan had formerly inhabited the land and done horrible things in it: so much so that God sent Israel against them under Joshua with orders to exterminate them. But now the Lord has to say through Jeremiah. 'A wonderful and horrible thing is committed in the land. The prophets prophesy falsely, and the priests bear rule by their means; and My people love to have it so; and what will ye do in the end thereof?' (Jeremiah 5:30-31). What God did through the Babylonian king 'in the end thereof', Jeremiah had to see and experience to his deep sorrow. We may get some idea of the depth of his grief, if we read the book of Lamentations, which follows his main prophecy.

This book is followed by Ezekiel who was carried amongst many others into captivity in the days of Jehoiachin some years before the final crash fell on Zedekiah, which Jeremiah witnessed. In the land of his captivity he saw in vision the glory, which marked the presence of God, departing from temple and city, and if God was gone, all was lost.

Yet each of these three prophets predicted God's future intervention in a way that would be altogether new. Isaiah foretold things that should be absolutely new, even, '*new* heavens and a *new* earth', brought about by the twofold advent of the Messiah; first as the humbled Servant, to suffer for sins, and then as the mighty Arm of Jehovah redeeming in power what He had first redeemed by His blood.

Jeremiah follows, predicting that these new things will be established, not on the old covenant of law but on a *new* covenant of grace. Let verses 31-34 of his 31st chapter be read and note how again and again, 'I will', appears, rather than the, 'If ye will', of Exodus 19:5. In this New Covenant, God is going to act according to His own thoughts and purposes in grace, based on the work of Christ, as unfolded by Isaiah.

Ezekiel completes the prophetic outline, that is given to us by these three major prophets. In his 36th chapter he foretells the *New* Birth that will take place with a remnant of Israel before they enter on millennial blessedness, and his next chapter speaks of how they will be spiritually quickened, and brought into a *new* order of life.

This brings us to Daniel, who was raised up by God just as the 'times of the Gentiles' (Luke 21:24) began under Nebuchadnezzar. He was enabled of God to give us a prophetic outline of the course of these times, during which the Messiah would be cut off. Hence tribulation is to be the portion of the people, but with the hope of deliverance at the end.

Daniel's prophecy falls quite simply into two parts after the introductory chapter, which relates the courageous stand of Daniel and his three companions against the taint of idolatry, and the way God honoured it. From the point where the Chaldeans spoke 'to the king in Syriack' (2:4), to the end of chapter 7, this language of the Gentiles is used, and Hebrew is only reverted to as we start chapter 8. Thus the historical details and the prophecies that relate to the Gentile powers are written in the Gentile language. Then in the five chapters that complete the book things are revealed to Daniel that mainly concern his people, though details as to the nations are referred to.

CHAPTER ONE

Three times did Nebuchadnezzar and his servants come up against Jerusalem, when the three kings, Jehoiakim, Jehoiachin and Zedekiah, fell before him. On the first of these occasions, Daniel and his three friends were carried captive amongst a number of youths of royal or princely birth, who were considered to be of exceptional intellectual capacity—the pick of the nation in wisdom and understanding. The astute Babylonian king intended to fortify his position with the cleverest men of conquered nations, working them into the army of magicians—the men who trafficked with demon powers, and gave him guidance by their occult practices.

So Daniel and his friends were to go through a kind of college course that would make them to be 'cunning in knowledge, and understanding science'; the 'science' being doubtless connected with those 'curious arts', mentioned in Acts 19:19, as practised in Ephesus at a later date. If the great Babylonian monarch could increase the number of men who could give him supernatural wisdom and guidance, his power would be further increased.

Hence their food and drink was to be of a special and prescribed course from the king's table: the very best of the land, and doubtless of a kind that was connected with idolatrous rites. And further, by the prince of the eunuchs each had his original name discarded. They had come under new ownership, and this was signalized by new names of idolatrous origin and significance. Such was the position in which Daniel and his companions found themselves.

Reaching verse 8 of chapter 1, our thoughts are arrested by the words, 'But Daniel purposed in his heart that he would not defile himself.' A great statement this! Had he not so purposed, no Book of Daniel would have found a place in our Bibles. Notice in the first place that the Spirit of God in the record disowns his heathen name, and uses his original one, which means, 'God is Judge'. The man evidently lived in the light of his name, and so we notice, in the second place, that he purposed, not in his head, the seat of intelligence, but rather in his heart, the seat of affection Godward, before whom he walked. This is the kind of purpose that stands firm and does not vary.

Then, in the third place, notice that it was *defilement* that he was determined to avoid. From a material standpoint the food was pure without a doubt. It was the spiritual defilement he had in view, since Babylon was the original hot-bed of idolatry. His three friends are not mentioned in verse 8, but if we turn to verse 18 of chapter 3, we discover they were entirely of the same mind and purpose as he was.

Let us take very seriously to heart the lesson that confronts us here. The secret of Daniel's remarkable power was his *purposed separation* from the evil world that surrounded him. He knew its defiling power and he refused it. Some five centuries after his day its true character was fully and finally exposed in the cross of Christ as He Himself said, 'Now is the judgment of this world' (John 12:31). We now live in the light of this fact, and we know that it is dominated by Satan, who is 'the god of this world' (2 Corinthians 4:4); hence a purposed separation from the world is more necessary for us than it was even for Daniel.

There was with him however not only great firmness of purpose but also a wise and humble spirit in making it known. God had acted on his behalf, bringing him into favour with the prince of the eunuchs and with Melzar his subordinate, yet he did not presume on this and speak haughtily. He rather stated his desire, and presented his prayer that he and his friends might be fed on the plainest of food for ten days as a test, and on the result of this the situation should be stabilized. God was with them and as a result they were delivered from the defilement that otherwise would have been theirs.

From this incident let us learn a lesson. Separation from defilement is ever God's path for His saints, but much depends on the spirit they display as they take it. If taken in a harsh or haughty spirit, rather than a meek and lowly spirit, the testimony to others will be nullified. If our spirit in taking it is marked by, 'Stand by thyself, come not near to me; for I am holier than thou'—the spirit that marked the Pharisees of our Lord's day—we shall be helping on the evil from which we profess to be separating ourselves. Daniel and his friends sought their separation, and maintained it, in the right spirit.

Consequently God was with them in a truly remarkable way. Not only were they fairer and fatter in their bodies, but in knowledge, skill, learning, wisdom they excelled all the others who had their portion of the king's meat; and as for Daniel, he was granted a supernatural understanding in visions and dreams, by which in those days God often made His mind known.

When tested before Nebuchadnezzar the verdict was clear. The magicians and astrologers were men who trafficked with the powers of darkness in order to possess knowledge beyond the powers of ordinary men, and compared with these the four men, taught of God, were ten times better. There is nothing surprising in this. Indeed the same thing meets us in more emphatic form in 1 Corinthians 2, where we read that the princes of this world knew nothing of God's wisdom, so much so that they 'crucified the Lord of glory'. Whereas the simplest believer, indwelt and controlled by the Spirit of God, judges, or discerns, 'all things'.

Before passing from chapter 1, we may remark that this question of food contaminated by idolatrous practices was acute among the early Christians at Corinth. They were instructed as to it in Paul's first epistle to them, chapters 8 and 10:25-31. Meat sold in the markets or supplied in a friend's house they could eat without raising any question; but if they were definitely informed that it had been offered in sacrifice to idols, they were to have none of it. In this the Christian keeps clear of idolatrous associations just as Daniel and his friends did.

CHAPTER TWO

With the sensational rise of Babylon under Nebuchadnezzar the times of the Gentiles began, and chapter 2 opens with the statement that as early as his second year that great monarch had a remarkable dream that troubled him much; and well it might, for in it lay a God-given revelation calculated to humble him. He lost his sleep and, what to him was worse, he lost also any recollection of his dream. He turned naturally to the Chaldeans and their associates, who trafficked with demon powers; demanding that they should recount his dream as well as give its meaning.

This demand, with the threat that, if they failed to answer to it, they should all be destroyed, does at first sight seem savage and unreasonable. On second thoughts we may remember that just about that time there were false prophets and diviners even in Jerusalem, as we see in Jeremiah 29, whose predictions and explanations failed, and so it doubtless had been with the diviners of Babylon. Nebuchadnezzar may have thought he had now a fine opportunity to test these men that surrounded him, and would wish to control him with supernatural understanding as they claimed. If they claimed to give supernatural interpretation of dreams, surely the same supernatural power could reconstruct the forgotten dream! This would verify the claims they made. And if they could not verify their claims, he would wipe them out of his kingdom!

Daniel and his friends being classified by the Babylonians as being amongst these 'wise men', they were included in the decree issued by the furious king. The action of Daniel and his friends is instructive. They did two things. First, there was Daniel's humble supplication to the king for time, with the assurance that an answer would be forthcoming. This assurance revealed *faith in God* on the part of Daniel, and that of very remarkable strength. Second, having obtained this brief respite, Daniel and his fellows gave themselves to *prayer* that the secret as to the dream might be revealed to them.

So here were these four men, surrounded by the grossest form of idolatry in the world's greatest city, yet so truly separated in heart and ways from it all as to be in touch with the 'God of heaven', to the point of receiving communications from Him. The secret they prayerfully sought was revealed to Daniel in a night vision. He saw by night just what the king had seen by night some days before. Others had been enabled to interpret dreams—Joseph for instance—but to duplicate a dream, so that what appeared before the mind of one man by night should be exactly repeated before the mind of another man a few nights later; this none can achieve but **God**. And in no servant of His does God perform this miracle but in one who was thoroughly separated to Him from the defilements of the surrounding world.

The first thing that Daniel did was to bless God and offer praise to Him, as shown in verses 19-23. He was indeed living in an epoch when God had been changing 'the times and the seasons', and also removing kings, and setting up kings, showing that wisdom and might are His. The removing of the kings of David's line and the setting up of Nebuchadnezzar had been acts of God, and Daniel bowed to this and even blessed God in the acknowledgment of it. He blessed God too that He imparted wisdom to those who had been given understanding to receive it, and in particular that the desired secret had been made known unto him.

'Times and seasons' as relating to the earth are first mentioned in Genesis 1:14. We have the exact words here, and we meet with them again in Acts 1:7 and 1 Thessalonians 5:1. It is clear that this expression refers to God's dispensations and dealings *on the earth*. In Acts 1, the disciples were *not to know* the *time* of God's dealings. Yet the Thessalonians *did know* the *manner* of God's predicted dealings, and the order in which they would transpire: indeed they knew this *perfectly*, though they were ignorant of the coming of the Lord for His saints, as revealed in the previous chapter. But then, that coming has to do with a *heavenly* calling, while 'times and seasons' relate to the *earth*.

The dream being revealed, Daniel is quickly brought before the king, and at once disclaims any virtue as resident in himself. He referred the king to the God of heaven, who reveals secrets, and who intends to make known to him the future course of Gentile dominion, that had commenced with his overthrow of Jerusalem and its king. Nebuchadnezzar was plainly told that God had thus acted for the sake of Daniel himself and his fellows, and that he might realize that he had to do with a God who knew the most secret thoughts of his heart and mind. In verses 31-35, the dream is related to the king.

We pass on however to consider the dream, as its meaning is unfolded by Daniel, beginning with verse 37. The golden head of this great image of excellent and terrible brightness was Nebuchadnezzar himself. He wielded absolute power, unfettered and unlimited, as no one before had known, nor has anyone since, and which we believe will only be equalled by the predicted 'Beast' of Revelation 13, and exceeded by the Lord Jesus, when He comes as King of kings and Lord of lords. The Lord Jesus will judge and rule in equity, but it was far otherwise with Nebuchadnezzar, for, 'whom he would he slew; and whom he would he kept alive' (5:19), as Daniel himself recorded.

The Babylonian empire, magnificent as it was, only dominated the stage in the world's history for a short time. Under Belshazzar and his father it fell from its proud pre-eminence. It was so much dependent upon the power and glory of Nebuchadnezzar that no subsequent king is regarded, and in verse 39 we read, 'after thee shall arise another kingdom' which was to be inferior in its character, described in the dream by the breast and arms of silver; and this again superseded by a third kingdom, designated by the belly and thighs of brass.

The lessening value of the metals indicated a deterioration in the quality of the succeeding powers. We may think it a hard saying, but autocracy is the Divine ideal in government, to be realized in righteous yet benevolent perfection in the millennial reign of Christ. It is worthy of note that in this chapter Daniel more than once speaks of 'the God of heaven', indicating that this first Gentile monarch of supreme power held his authority as delegated from heaven. This is the fact, we believe, that underlies the instruction of the Apostle given in Romans 13:1. The existing power of his day was the fourth, mentioned in our chapter, but the Gentile powers that exist, whoever they may be at any given moment, hold their authority as delegates of 'the God of heaven'.

The second and third empires are passed over with slight mention and our thoughts are concentrated on the fourth, which was to be characterized by strength, as set forth by the iron. The Roman empire did indeed break in pieces and subdue the civilized earth, and lasted in its unified form for centuries. Though its unity was dissolved, as we know, it is viewed in the dream as existing in some way until its final development in a ten-kingdom form at the end of its story, when clay will be found mixed with the iron; and in result the kingdom will be partly strong and partly brittle.

The mixture of clay and iron aptly symbolizes this, for they are substances entirely different in character. Iron is a metal, of less value than gold, though stronger: clay is non-metallic, and its figurative use in Scripture indicates what is human in contrast to what is Divine: see Job 10:9 and 33:6; also the references to man being like clay in the hands of God, who is the Potter.

The dream indicated therefore that the fourth empire in its last days would have 'kings', to the number of ten, and that though still strong there would be an element of brittleness, induced by the introduction of a human element—what in these days we call democracy; which was defined by a noted man as being, 'Government of the *people* by the *people* for the *people*'. Nothing is more uncertain, and therefore brittle, than the will of the *people*. It seems quite certain therefore that we are living in the days contemplated as being the closing stage in the history of the image.

Upon the feet of the image the stone fell. The stone is described as 'cut out without hands'; that is, apart from man having anything to do with it—not human but Divine in origin. The first prophetic reference to the Lord Jesus as the Stone is in Genesis 49:24, when old Jacob, in blessing his sons made a parenthetic exclamation, 'from thence is the Shepherd, the Stone of Israel'. Under this figure He again appears in Isaiah 28:16, and so on into the New Testament.

In the dream we are considering, the stone is interpreted as 'A kingdom, which shall never be destroyed', but we know who the King of that kingdom is going to be. Just as the 'vision' of Habakkuk 2:3, which will surely come and not tarry, is found in Hebrews 10:37 to be centred in a Person, (for the 'it' of Habakkuk is turned into 'He' in Hebrews), so the 'kingdom' which Daniel mentioned as predicted by the 'stone' of Nebuchadnezzar's dream is found to centre round a Person, who is God's 'King of kings'.

We know Him as the 'Living Stone', and to Him we have already come, as we are reminded in 1 Peter 2:4-5. We are His already and we partake of His nature as 'living stones', and so are built up, as under His authority, into that spiritual house and holy priesthood, as indicated. When as the King of that coming kingdom, predicted in Daniel 2, He falls in judgment it will be completely to *demolish*. While we wait for that, we know His attractive power, the effect of which is to *build up*. How great the favour and blessing of knowing Him thus!

It is indeed a solemn thought that judgment has at last to fall on the imposing image, that represents Gentile dominion on earth, and crush all to powder. It should have a sobering effect on us all, as we realize that *nothing* of all man's pomp and power and outward glory is going to remain. Not only are the iron and clay ground to powder, but the gold and silver and brass also. The wind of God will sweep all away as chaff. The God, who will do this, is **great**, and He was making it known to this king, who was great in the eyes of men. The greatness of God guaranteed the certainty of the things the dream foretold.

This should remind us of what we read in 1 Corinthians 1:19 and 2:6, where the Apostle's words inform us that not only powerful Gentile kingdoms are to be swept away, but that also the intellectual princes of the earth and all the wisdom they represent will come to *nothing* in the day when God rises up in judgment.

This revelation, that reached the king through Daniel, had an immediate effect upon him, as we see in the closing verses of the chapter. Instead of being angered by this prediction of ultimate disaster, he was made acutely conscious that he was in the presence of the supernatural—a power was in evidence that he had found wholly wanting in the Chaldeans and his magicians. Only, true to his heathen upbringing, he was mainly concerned with the man in whom the power was displayed. He did indeed acknowledge that Daniel's God was 'a God of gods, and a Lord of kings', but the worship he offered was directed to Daniel, rather than to the God in whose name he spoke. So we see here an illustration of what is written in Romans 1:25, that the heathen 'worshipped and served the creature more than the Creator, who is blessed for ever. Amen.'

So Daniel was not only worshipped but also made one of the chief, if not the very chief, of the advisers and rulers under the king, and at his request his three companions were also greatly elevated. They went at one bound, so to speak, into high positions of prominence. And did this wonderful display of Divine power have a salutary and lasting effect on Nebuchadnezzar? The next chapter shows quite conclusively that it did *not*.

CHAPTER THREE

How long an interval there was between the events narrated in chapters 2 and 3, we are not told, but we cannot resist the impression that there was a connection in the mind of Nebuchadnezzar between the image of his dream and the gigantic image, that he caused to be made. The image of his dream only began with a golden head, which represented himself. It was followed by a great image, which should be all of gold.

Since the ancient cubit was the length of the human fore-arm—anything from 18 to 22 inches—this image must have been at least 90 feet high, with a breadth of 9 feet. The immense store of gold, which enabled the king to do this, may not have equalled the supply that came to Solomon, yet it shows that the 'times of the Gentiles' began with a great display of power and wealth and glory. And how will the period of Gentile dominion end? The answer to this we find in Revelation 13. Another mighty king will arise, and another great image will be made. If we compare the two scenes, we note many resemblances, and yet a significant contrast; in the fact that, as we read in the last chapter, it was 'the God of Heaven' who gave to Nebuchadnezzar 'power and strength and glory'; whereas the coming great king, who is named 'the beast', will obtain 'his power, and his seat, and great authority' (Revelation 13:2), from 'the dragon'; that is, from the devil himself.

The resemblances are equally striking, and bear witness to the fact that the sinful tendencies of poor fallen man in all ages are just the same. By the God of Heaven Nebuchadnezzar was granted much power and glory, so at once he used it to glorify himself in this gigantic golden image. Many different peoples were under his sway, each with their many gods, whom they worshipped. Now let them, while retaining their local deities, have a kind of 'super-religion', which would have the effect of binding them together under his sway. Hence the cry of the herald, beginning, 'O people, nations, and languages'.

Moreover these ancient monarchs knew how to influence the masses. Music exerts a very subtle influence on the human mind. So, to move the mighty concourse of people to worship the golden image, and thus pay homage to the mighty king, 'all kinds of music' were played. The penalty for non-compliance was the dreadful one of being cast alive into a burning fiery furnace.

Very similar things are predicted in Revelation 13 for the end of the age, but with even more striking accompaniments. Instead of all kinds of music, the false prophet will have power to give life and speech to the image of the beast, and those who refuse to worship will be killed. The statement that there will be power to give 'life' to the image is indeed a startling one, but we must remember that at that time there will be 'the working of Satan with all power and signs and lying wonders, and with all deceivableness of unrighteousness in them that perish' (2 Thessalonians 2:9-10).

As we read on in our chapter, we learn how God changed Nebuchadnezzar's word and thwarted his determination. As we read on in Revelation, we learn in chapter 19 how far more drastic and eternal judgment, though longer delayed, will fall upon the beast, who is personified by the image that is to come, and on the false prophet, who will promote it.

Of all the lusts and desires that are resident in the nature of poor fallen man, the most deep-seated is the desire to glorify, even to the point of deifying, himself. At the outset he fell to the seductive assertion of Satan, 'Ye shall be as gods, knowing good and evil' (Genesis 3:5). The adversary did not of course state that they would know good, without being able to achieve it, and evil, without being able to avoid it. Ever since, self-exaltation has been the ruling idea in our world. Thus it was with Nebuchadnezzar. For the moment he was the apex of the pyramid, and beneath him, acting in his support, were 'the princes, the governors, and the captains, the judges, the treasurers, the counsellors, the sheriffs, and all the rulers of the provinces'; and this eight-fold description of important personages is given twice in our chapter, as if to impress us with the solidity of the pyramid of which he was the apex. From this apparently unchallengeable position the great king issued his decree, which was in effect a God-defying one. And God took up the challenge through three devoted servants that He had in reserve.

Remarkably enough Daniel is not mentioned in this chapter: a fact that should be of encouragement to us. Why not mentioned, and where he was, is not revealed;

but it is encouraging to know that in the absence of a servant of striking courage and power, God can take up and use with great effect servants of lesser gifts. Daniel's three companions did not possess his gifts of understanding as to dreams and prophecies, but they did share his devotion to the one true God, which entailed a thorough-going separation from the abomination of idolatry. Hence, when the multitudes from the highest to the least fell down to worship the image, they stood erect. They exemplified the principle stated by the apostles in Acts 5:29— 'We ought to obey God rather than man.'

Their enemies at once reported this to incite the rage and fury of Nebuchadnezzar. The king did at least enquire if the reported lack of action was true, and then issued his ultimatum, coupled with the insolent question, 'Who is that God that shall deliver you out of my hands?' The reply of the three Jews was a memorable one.

If memory serves us aright, this is the first case on record where a servant of God has been threatened with the direst form of death penalty, if he did not deny his God and forsake his faith, though a prophet like Elijah was threatened by Jezebel. There have been many such cases since. In chapter 6 we have the case of Daniel. In the history of the early church we read of many who were thrown to the wild beasts because they would not deny their Lord and Master. Many a 'heretic' went to the fires in our land, as well as in Spain under the Inquisition; and we believe not a few have done so in our day under the iron hand of Communism. But, as we have often noticed, the first case is a very memorable one, and the stand taken rings through the centuries.

In the first place they asserted that their God was able to deliver them. They exalted His power. In the second place they did not hide the fact that for reasons of His own He might not deliver them. And then, in the third place, they stated with the utmost decision that were He not pleased to deliver, they would **not** forsake their God by worshipping the king's golden image, in the honour of gods that were false. 'We will **not** serve thy gods', was their decisive word; and in result they were greatly honoured by their God.

We shall, however, do well to remember that the seductions of the world are more damaging to our testimony than its opposition and its threat of disaster or death. At the end of his life the Apostle Paul had to write, 'Demas hath forsaken me', and he did not follow this by saying, 'being fearful of the world's threatenings', but rather, 'having loved this present world' (2 Timothy 4:10). Paul had just before written of, 'all them also that love His appearing'; knowing that the appearing of the Lord Jesus will usher in a world very different from the present one, and that is wholly according to God. Demas fell before the seductions of the present 'world', or 'age', and that surely is the danger for us—the Christians of English-speaking lands, who are largely exempt from the persecutions experienced elsewhere. May God give us that decision of character that marked the three Hebrews, so that faced by seductions we may say, 'Be it known … that we will **not** …'.

Pursuing the narrative, we note the complete change in Nebuchadnezzar, as compared with the picture presented at the end of chapter 2. Then he was on his face in the presence of Daniel, and to fall on one's face is to efface oneself in a figurative way. Now he is on his feet and so full of fury that his very face was transformed with savage resolution. Not only are the three men, who have defied his will, to be thrust into the fire, but the furnace is to be seven times hotter than what was the ordinary thing. As a consequence the mightiest men of his army were to fling them in. Thus the judgment fell. The deed was done.

And then the hand of God began to appear. The judgment fell, but it was upon the most mighty of Nebuchadnezzar's famous army, and not upon the three defenceless Jews. The first thing the proud, impious king saw was his mightiest men slain by the furnace he had so excessively heated up. A humiliating sight for him! The next thing he saw was four men walking, free and unhurt in the midst of the fire, the very outskirts of which had slain his finest soldiers. The fire, that was death to them, was not only preservation but liberty to God's servants. They were flung in 'bound', but now they 'walk', for the only things consumed were their bonds, and they had a heavenly Visitor with them.

In the presence of this astounding miracle the furious king was subdued. The dream of chapter 2, which Daniel had expounded, had moved him, but though he learned that he was the golden head of the dream image, he had not taken to heart the fact that the supreme earthly position that he had reached was granted to him by 'the God of heaven'. If he had, he would never have boastfully asked, Who was the God that could deliver out of his hands? The God of heaven, who had given him his dominion, had accepted his challenge, reversed his word, quenched the violence of his seven-fold heated fire, and made visible His presence with those who were to have been his victims.

The king recognized that there was something Divine and God-like about 'the form of the fourth'. The way in which he expressed his conviction was doubtless controlled by God. Before this, Balaam had said things that he never would have uttered apart from Divine compulsion. After this, Caiaphas uttered things that had a different meaning to that which he intended, as recorded in John 11:51. So it was here. Nebuchadnezzar recognized that God had intervened and manifested His presence with the men he had sought to slay, and he used just the right expression, though not understanding the true force of it. While it is the Father who forms the purpose, it is the Son who manifests and acts. This we learn when the New Testament is reached.

The miracle was so complete that their garments were not affected, not an hair of their heads singed, not even the smell of fire was attached to them. The king had fully to recognize the hand of God, and acknowledged His mighty power. Still he did not advance beyond knowing Him as 'the God of Shadrach, Meshach, and Abednego', just as at the end of chapter 2 he acknowledged Him as the God of Daniel. He did not acknowledge Him as *his* God, though he pronounced severe penalties against any who spoke against Him. This great man, with whom the times of the Gentiles began, had yet a deeper lesson to learn.

CHAPTER FOUR

This we find as we read on into chapter 4, where a remarkable change in the narration takes place. We are permitted to read what, at a later date, Nebuchadnezzar himself caused to be written and published to all the many nations and languages that were beneath his sway. In it he made known the dealings of God—whom he now called 'the Most High God' (New Trans.)—with himself personally. It was a story of his own complete discomfiture and humiliation at the hands of God; and therefore the very fact, that he should publish the story abroad, indicated a great and fundamental change in his own mind and attitude.

The preface to his story, and especially verse 3, is very striking. He mentions first 'His signs' and 'His wonders'. We live in an age that is characterized by faith. The Apostle Paul could write of a time, 'before faith came', and again of a time, 'after that faith is come' (Galatians 3:23, 25). Signs that appealed to sight had a special place before the epoch of faith began. But it is also a fact that, when God inaugurated a fresh dispensation, He authenticated what is new by signs of a miraculous nature. It was so when He brought Israel out of Egypt; and the law epoch began at Sinai. It was so in supreme fashion when He manifested Himself in His Son the Lord Jesus Christ; and again when the church age began, as we see in the Acts of the Apostles. So it was, as we see here, when the times of the Gentiles began.

The particular sign and wonder that Nebuchadnezzar is now about to relate is, as we see, very humbling to himself. In one hour his mighty kingdom departed from him, though presently restored. In contrast to this, he confessed God's kingdom to be everlasting. Though he may not have in any full measure realized it, two or three generations would see his dominion, typified by gold, fall before another dominion, typified by silver. God's kingdom, he acknowledged, abides through all generations. This he confessed before he narrated the experience that made him realize it. God had to act toward him in judgment.

Before acting, God issued a warning. This is ever His way. There was warning through Noah before the flood. There was warning for Pharaoh before the judgments on Egypt. There was warning for Jerusalem through Jeremiah before the city fell to the Babylonians. There is warning today as to the judgments that will fall when the church age is closed. So it was here with this powerful individual. God warned him by means of a dream. His first dream might well have lifted him up, for he was the head of gold. His second dream warned him of a complete casting down.

The warning came just when the king seemed to have reached the very climax of his prosperity. His many warlike expeditions were over; his great conquests completed. He was at last at rest and flourishing in the palace of his magnificent city. As we all know, dreams are strange and unaccountable things. As sleep fades, and the mind begins to resume its activities, unusual things may flit across its awakening consciousness. It is not surprising therefore that God has been pleased to make known His thoughts and purposes to men by means of a dream, especially in times of urgency and importance. It is remarkable, for instance, that in the first two chapters of Matthew's Gospel, we get God speaking in a dream no less than five times.

As the result of his second dream Nebuchadnezzar was again troubled and afraid. He was conscious that it proceeded from the unseen world, and had in it a message for him; yet God's previous dealings with him had left no permanent impression, for in his trouble he again thought first of the magicians of various kinds and the Chaldeans, and when they failed, Daniel was brought in as a last resort.

We notice, however, that though Daniel was consulted, the king addressed him under the heathen name that had been given him. In both verses 8 and 9 we find, 'Belteshazzar', which he states was 'according to the name of my god', for Bel was one of the great gods of Babylon. Moreover, in keeping with the heathen name that he used, he only recognized that in Daniel was, 'the spirit of the holy gods'. The true God— 'the God of Heaven', —who had given to him his great dominion, was as yet unknown to him.

This we have, be it remembered, by his own confession, before he proceeded to relate the dream, which made him afraid, warning him of the blow that was impending from the hand of God.

In verses 10-17, we have Nebuchadnezzar's own account of the dream that made him afraid. We have only to read these verses to see that there was in it a strongly marked element of the supernatural. Not only was there a visitation from 'a Watcher and an Holy One', but also a decree, endorsed by 'the Most High', who 'ruleth in the kingdom of men'. The king could only turn to Daniel, addressing him as *Bel*teshazzar, 'according to the name of my god'. The Babylonian gods are mentioned satirically in Isaiah 46:1, '*Bel* boweth down, *Nebo* stoopeth'. So, though he hoped for enlightenment from a man, 'in whom is the spirit of the holy gods', we are not surprised that before the Most High he was afraid.

In verse 19 we see that Daniel himself, to whom the meaning of the dream was at once revealed, was also afraid and troubled, for he realized it warned the king of impending chastisement from the hand of God—a stroke of the severest kind.

Let us briefly review what had preceded this dream. The times of the Gentiles began when Nebuchadnezzar reached the zenith of human splendour, wielding autocratic power in unparalleled fashion. By an earlier dream he had been warned that though he was the head of gold in the great image, deterioration would set in, and at the end the dominion, vested temporarily in him, would be crushed to powder under the judgment of God.

How little this affected him we see in the next chapter. The dearest passion in the heart of fallen man is that of self-exaltation. So the great king has made the gigantic image, which all are to worship, and woe betide him who does not! Again God intervened. He gave courage to three of His servants, who braved the king's wrath and his furnace, though seven-times heated. In result, Nebuchadnezzar was defeated. God simply made a fool of him in the presence of vast crowds of his peoples. Had this any permanent effect upon him for good?

The chapter we are considering shows that it had not. He is still the same self-glorifying man. Consequently God will act in an even more drastic way. The first intervention was addressed to his intelligence—his understanding of the future. The second was a display of the Divine power, which publicly humiliated him. Still no permanent alteration, though for the moment he was deeply impressed. So now the kingdom of 'gold' will be left intact, while he alone is dealt with.

This second dream concerned a great tree. Elsewhere in Scripture great men and nations are likened to imposing trees—Ezekiel 31, for instance—so the figure was not an unusual one. Daniel at once saw that the king himself was portrayed, and the judgment that was to fall on him.

God will not strike him personally until warning has been given. This indeed is ever His kindly way. He did not send the flood on the world of the ungodly until ample warning had been given; nor captivity upon Israel until they had been fully warned by the prophets. Today we live in an age very near to judgment, as to which warning has long been given. Are we sufficiently aware of this? When the Gospel of grace is preached, is the note of warning sounded with sufficient clearness? We sadly fear that it is not, but rather avoided as an unpleasant theme.

The warning given today may be disregarded by most, even as it was by Nebuchadnezzar. Daniel courageously warned him and even counselled him to alter his ways, as we see in verse 27. But the warning given was not heeded, nor the counsel given followed. Even then, God waited twelve months before His judgment fell.

Walking amidst the splendours of Babylon, the king experienced a moment of supreme pride. Everything around him spoke of his 'power', his 'honour', his 'majesty'. The ruins of Babylon are remarkable even today, and men of understanding have reconstructed in picture form the marvels they must have contained. As we looked at the picture, we could only say that if it was at all accurate then none of our present cities could rival it. The king filled with pride, felt himself to be exalted above measure. Then the blow fell.

From a pinnacle of glory Nebuchadnezzar was now degraded to the level of a beast, indeed almost beneath that level; and in that miserable, bestial condition 'seven times' passed over him. It was no passing affliction but a protracted one, though it is not indicated here whether 'times' means years. Elsewhere apparently, it does.

An element of prophecy enters, we believe, into this story, for it is a remarkable fact that a 'beast' appears at the end of the record concerning Gentile dominion, when we come to Revelation 13. The last man who will hold that supreme place, and who will be crushed by the appearing of the Lord Jesus in His glory, is described as a 'beast'. He will not be a demented one, as was Nebuchadnezzar, but he will be worse because dominated by Satan, never lifting up his eyes to heaven but always down to the earth. And further, if we are right in identifying him with 'the prince that shall come' of Daniel 9:26-27, his career will cover the 'week' of years, mentioned in those verses—the equivalent of 'seven times'.

There is a contrast, however, for the beast of the last days goes to his doom in 'a lake of fire burning with brimstone', whereas Nebuchadnezzar at the end of his seven times was restored to sanity and to his kingdom. And further, this time something effectual does seem to have been wrought in his soul. Not only did he lift up his eyes to heaven with the understanding of a man but he blessed God, giving Him His title of 'the Most High'. Now the first time that this great name of God occurs is in Genesis 14, where Melchizedek is called a priest of 'the Most High God' who is therefore, 'Possessor of heaven and earth'.

Some understanding of this fact had now entered the heart of Nebuchadnezzar, as we see in verses 34 and 35. This opened the king's eyes to the fact of his own nothingness, for he confessed that, 'all the inhabitants of the earth are reputed as nothing'; and if **all**, then himself among them. He recognized also the supreme power of God in enforcing His will in heaven and on earth. In the presence of the greatness and the power of God, he at last recognized his own nothingness and impotence.

At last Nebuchadnezzar had learned his lesson, and made public acknowledgment of the God of heaven, and therefore the discipline of very severe sort, through which he had been passed, was removed and he was restored to his kingdom in a chastened spirit. His public confession and praise of 'the King of heaven', is recorded in the last verse of our chapter. To Him he ascribed 'honour', 'truth' and 'judgement' in all His dealings. Never had a man been more lifted up in pride than this king, and never had a proud man been more signally abased.

Let us not forget the abasing power of God. We often dwell upon the grace of Christ, as mentioned in the Epistle to the Hebrews, but let us not forget that not only is He able to sympathize, 'able to succour', and 'able to save', but also, 'able to abase'. He did it effectually with Nebuchadnezzar, and evidently for his spiritual good. He will presently do it far more drastically with the 'beast' of Revelation 13, as we see when chapter 19 of that book is reached. The pride of man, generated by his scientific advances and consequent wonderful achievements, is increasing. It will reach its climax ere long. Then Nebuchadnezzar's confession will be demonstrated as true in overwhelming fashion— 'those that walk in pride He is able to abase.'

CHAPTER FIVE

The period of Babylonian supremacy was comparatively brief, and the 'head of gold' had to give place to the 'breast and arms of silver'. As we begin to read chapter 5, we find ourselves transported to the last hours of that period. The great city was still marked by scenes of wealth and much voluptuous splendour.

Years ago, learned critics claimed that the Book of Daniel was largely legendary and written several centuries after the events it related. Belshazzar, they regarded as an imaginary figure, since they found no reference to him in extant records. Later, however, his name did appear on a clay tablet that was unearthed, so this assertion, like a great many more of their unbelieving assertions, was shattered as the archaeologists dug in these ancient ruins. It appears that in accordance with an ancient custom he was associated with his father in the kingship, and that his father being elsewhere at that time, he was virtually king in Babylon just as it fell before the rising power of Medo-Persia.

Whatever may have been the permanent effect upon Nebuchadnezzar of God's dealings with him, his successors displayed all the arrogant splendour of his earlier years. Belshazzar's name began with the name of Babylon's god; the gorgeous feast with a thousand of his lords, together with wives and concubines was typically heathenish. Inflamed by wine, he had the golden vessels, that had years before been taken from the temple in Jerusalem, brought before them, so that gloating over them, they might publicly dishonour Jehovah, and praise their many false gods of metals, of wood and of stone. He deliberately flung down the gauntlet before God, who at once accepted the challenge.

This, we believe, is always God's way. He does not act in judgment until the evil is fully manifested. It was so with the Amorite nations, as shown in Genesis 15:16. It was so with the kings and people in Jerusalem, as testified in 2 Chronicles 36:11-20. It will be so again in the sad history of Christendom, as predicted in Revelation 17 and 18.

Thus it was in that great festive hall in Babylon, and in result we have one of the most dramatic scenes on record. No legion of angels appeared, no visible display of Divine power: just the fingers as of a man's hand were visible, writing four words on the 'plaister of the wall', just 'over against the candlestick', where they were most visible. The proud king was reduced to a shivering mortal, and his lords astonished.

As we ponder this scene our thoughts turn in two directions. They travel back to Exodus, where we read of the law being given, written with 'the finger of God' upon tables of stone. It was fitting material for stone cannot be twisted or bent, though it can be broken. Here the finger of God is connected with demand upon guilty men. Then our thoughts travel on to John 8, where the guilty woman was brought by conceited Scribes and Pharisees to the Lord Jesus for condemnation. He did not condemn her: and why? Well, He gave an indication of the reason by stooping to write on the ground, and this He did twice, as if for emphasis. He stooped to write in the dust of the temple, for He had stooped from the heights of His glory, 'into the dust of death' (Psalm 22:15), so that the righteousness of God might be maintained and His love fully expressed. Here then we have not the finger of *demand*, but rather, as we may say, the finger of *dust*.

But now in Daniel we again have 'the finger of God', and we find it to be the finger of *doom*, written on plaster, that easily crumbles. God manifested His presence by showing the tip of His fingers, and it scared the life out of Belshazzar. When the final hour of judgment arrives and 'the dead, small and great, stand before God' (Revelation 20:12), what will be their feelings? We are reminded of that word, 'It is a fearful thing to fall into the hands of the living God' (Hebrews 10:31).

Once more the wise men of Babylon were called in, but only to display again incompetence and ignorance. We are told that there was nothing unusual about the four words. They were not words taken from some unknown, barbaric tongue, but, being on that occasion God's words, they were quite outside the understanding of these servants of the world and its false gods. The fact, stated by the Apostle Paul in 1 Corinthians 2:14, is strikingly illustrated. As 'natural' men they had no power of understanding the things God had written.

The whole scene was now transformed. Belshazzar had moved from profanity to prostration, and the whole company had descended from gaiety to gloom. Into this chaotic scene came 'the queen', as stated in verse 10, and in the next verse she refers to Nebuchadnezzar as 'father' of Belshazzar. Not infrequently 'father' is used in Scripture for 'forefather', and thus clearly it was here. She was evidently the queen-mother, and most likely a daughter of Nebuchadnezzar, and consequently possessing a much clearer remembrance of God's dealings with her father, as well as of Daniel and his God-given understanding.

What is quite evident is that, years having passed, Daniel had dropped completely out of public notice. In court circles his name was so unknown that the queen had to give a full account of him and of his powers, though she still treated them as being 'the wisdom of the gods'. Daniel is lifted from his obscurity, brought before the king and promised great honours if he could interpret the words. The reason why he was promised the *third* place in the kingdom was evidently because Belshazzar himself was only the *second*. The *first* being his father, who was at that moment elsewhere.

Daniel's answer, recorded in verse 17, is very striking. Previously, as recorded at the end of chapter 2, Daniel had accepted the honours placed upon him, now he treated them with disdain. The meaning of the four fateful words had evidently already penetrated to his heart, and he knew that Belshazzar was rejected of God, and his kingdom about to crash in ruin, so his proffered honours were worthless.

Before the interpretation of the words, God gave through Daniel the clearest indictment of the Babylonian empire, as summed up in Belshazzar, the existing head of it. The king was reminded of God's dealing with Nebuchadnezzar, which humbled him. Belshazzar had knowledge of this but had ignored it, and had exalted himself even more blatantly against 'the Lord of Heaven', by bringing the golden vessels that had been in the temple, where once His presence had been manifested, and glorying over Him, in praising the demon powers that were represented by his idols. This brought things to a climax, and the first of the 'overturnings', predicted in Ezekiel 21:27, was at hand.

By the writing on the wall a warning was given, though only a few hours were to elapse before the blow fell. The word '**numbered**' was twice written, as if it was a point to be emphasized. The God who can number the stars, as well as the hairs on a human head, had observed and numbered the proud sins of the Babylonian empire. The word '**weighed**' showed that Belshazzar himself had been tested and condemned. By 'divided', the immediate overthrow of the empire was announced.

The warning produced no change in Belshazzar, for he invested Daniel with honours, as though his kingdom was to continue, and that in spite of Daniel having renounced them. He wore those honours for just a few brief hours, for that night the predicted judgment fell. Darius the Median took the city and the kingdom, and Belshazzar was slain.

Thus came to its end the first of the great empires that are to fill up the times of the Gentiles. It gives us, we judge, a sample of the way in which God has caused the others to be overthrown; though the fourth, the Roman, is to be revived, and its component parts brought together again, that it may decisively and finally be destroyed by the personal appearing of the Lord Jesus, since it was under the Roman that He was mocked and crucified. Then it is that man's great empires will all of them together, be blown into nothingness, 'like the chaff of the summer threshingfloors'. When the writer was young it looked as if there was to be a stable British 'empire', for about a century ago the late Queen Victoria, of happy memory, had been proclaimed 'Empress of India'. A short century has proved that the term, 'empire', was a misnomer, and the word has been dropped.

CHAPTER SIX

The Medo-Persian empire now became the dominant world power, and Darius became king in Babylon. It appears that historians have difficulty in identifying this man. It may be that he was only a vassal king, under the suzerainty of Cyrus king of Persia; but this is a matter that need not detain us. In the Babylonian section of the new empire he arranged things as he saw fit, and again we find Daniel promoted to a place of great power. The hand of God was in it, though on the human side two things may have been in his favour. First, he was not a native of Babylon. Second, Darius almost certainly would have heard of the dramatic scene in the palace, just before he captured the city that seemed so impregnable, and thus of Daniel's superhuman understanding.

The scene brought before us in chapter 6 is very true to human life and nature. Daniel's exalted position filled the hearts of lesser men with envy and hatred. If possible, they would destroy him. This purpose of theirs brings to light a remarkable testimony as to his character— 'he was faithful, neither was there any error or fault found in him.' As a result they concluded that no attack on him would succeed unless it were made concerning the law of God.

Here we must pause, and consider our own ways. What point of attack does each one of us present to those who in an antagonistic spirit survey us critically? Very frequently, we fear, we present more points than one. Hence the constant exhortations to a life of godliness that we find in the Pauline epistles. To the Philippians, for instance, he urged, 'that ye may be blameless and harmless, the sons of God, without rebuke, in the midst of a crooked and perverse nation, among whom ye shine as lights in the world; holding forth the word of life' (Philippians 2:15-16). If we today, as well as the Philippians nineteen centuries ago, can be thus described, crooked and perverse folk who wish to accuse us will have to base their attack on the word of life, or the way in which we hold it forth, rather than on our personal ways. Let us each be very much exercised as to this matter.

The presidents and princes were shrewd men. They knew the power of flattery and how men love to exalt themselves. Hence they suggested to Darius a decree of self-exaltation; practically deifying himself for the period of a month. Into this trap Darius fell, and we learn in connection with it that in this kingdom of 'silver' the power of the monarch was not so absolute as in the kingdom of 'gold'. Nebuchadnezzar did just what he liked without curb laid upon him. The Medo-Persian kings had to consider their captains' and counsellors' advice, and a law, when once promulgated, could not be altered. The law was signed, by which under pain of a terrible death, any who feared the God of heaven, should be cut off from Him for thirty days. In principle he was doing again the great sin, attempted in chapter 3. Nebuchadnezzar demanded worship through his golden image. The method of Darius was far less spectacular, but equally against God. For all practical purposes there shall be no God but Darius for thirty days!

In chapter 3, Daniel is absent, and courage was given to his companions to stand firm in their allegiance to the one true God, and refuse to bow down to the image. In the present chapter the three companions are absent and Daniel alone is seen. Exactly the same spirit is seen in him. They would not for one moment bow down to worship a god of man's devising. He would not for one day cease to pray to the true God, whom he knew. They acted negatively, defying the king's command to worship Satanic powers. He acted positively, maintaining contact with the God of heaven, though it involved defying the command of Darius. In both cases

God stepped in, and miraculously sustained and delivered His servants in a way that exposed the folly of the kings.

Darius indeed was quickly made to discover his folly. Daniel made no sensational protest; he only went on doing what had been his custom. Three times each day he knelt before God with thanksgiving and prayer, and he made no secret of it, since he did it with windows open, and thus all could see.

But why did he have his windows open 'toward Jerusalem'? Read 1 Kings 8:46-50, and the reason is plain. He believed God would answer that petition in Solomon's prayer, so he fulfilled the stipulation that the prayer should be made, 'toward their land … the city which Thou hast chosen'. Such was the record in the Scriptures. In obedience he fulfilled it, and went on fulfilling it in spite of the king's decree.

Let us seriously ask ourselves if we are as observant of Scripture as Daniel, and moved by it to obedience as he was.

His courage has become almost proverbial. 'Dare to be a Daniel!' has become a well-known phrase. Good advice it is. But what gave him the courage to dare? The answer surely is—his reliance on God and His word. We may safely affirm that, down to our own time, all the saints who have acquired courage to stand for the truth, and suffer for it, have been fortified in the same way. In the tolerant, easy-going lands where English is spoken, compromise is the fashionable thing. But this was not Daniel's way, and should not be ours.

Hence, though 'an excellent spirit' was in Daniel, the jealous 'princes', who were under him, had no difficulty in denouncing him to the king, who foolishly and blasphemously had signed the decree, which could not be altered or revoked. Realizing his folly, the king made desperate attempts until nightfall to release Daniel, and incidentally himself, from the entanglement, which he himself had created. But all in vain.

So, just as in chapter 3, we saw the three faithful Hebrews going to their doom, now we see Daniel going to his. And with the same result. God intervened; altering the order of nature, and delivering His servant. Here we have a miracle equally remarkable with that recorded in chapter 3. God has established a certain order in creation, whether in the action of fire or that of living animals. Fire will uniformly burn clothes and even human bodies that wear them. Hungry wild beasts, such as lions, will uniformly spring upon and devour their prey. God, who has established this order, can reverse it, should it please Him so to do. It did please Him to do so in both cases. And His control of the lions in this case is equally remarkable with His suspension of the action of fire.

Some may wish to enquire why God has not acted in this way on behalf of His servants far more frequently? The answer surely is, that God acts in this *miraculous* way at the beginning of some change in His dealings with men, though He may often act on behalf of His saints in a *providential* way. It was so, for instance, at the beginning of the Christian dispensation. Peter was miraculously delivered from prison and death, as recorded in Acts 12. Since then, many a saint has died in prison for the sake of the Gospel, though some have been providentially delivered.

As we ponder over this, one reason for it at least becomes clear. In the two cases before us the times of the Gentiles had just begun by the complete overthrow of Israel and the destruction of Jerusalem. The natural conclusion to be deduced was that the gods of the Babylonian world were more powerful than Jehovah, whose temple was at Jerusalem. They were not, and God demonstrated it by these miraculous *deliverances* of His servants in the teeth of the powers of darkness. At the end of the age He will demonstrate it by the *damnation* of His foes, and theirs.

The same thing may be said of this present Gospel age. Acts 12, which begins with the deliverance of Peter, ends with the judgment of Herod. In both cases an angel 'smote'. He smote Peter *up* for deliverance, and then smote Herod *down* to a miserable and disgusting death. God has not repeated these actions, just because we live in this Gospel age, which is characterized by *grace*. When this age of grace ends, we shall see God's saints completely delivered, and their oppressors completely judged.

In Daniel 6 we see not only Daniel delivered but also the evil men, who conspired against him, judged. They and their families suffered the exact fate that they had designed for Daniel, and that by the order of the king they had deceived into the evil law.

The end of the chapter reveals the salutary effect of the whole episode on the mind of Darius. His confession and decree, which was sent so widely abroad, was similar to the edict sent forth previously by Nebuchadnezzar. Thus in the second of the four great world-empires this tribute to the One, confessed not only as 'the God of Daniel', but also as 'the living God, and stedfast for ever', was sent out to all men. The time had not come for the *love* of God to be manifested, but His *power* was declared in striking fashion, and everywhere men, under the sway of Darius, were commanded to 'tremble and fear' before Him.

Let us notice the 'decree' of verse 8, and by way of contrast, the 'decree' of verse 26. Both were issued in an empire that permitted no alteration or cancellation of its decrees, yet they do stand in contrast. The first was nullified as to its *penalty*; the second was soon nullified as to its *performance*. The subsequent history of that empire shows that men did **not** tremble and fear before the living God, as they were commanded to do. No empire can legislate in the things of God; and so this 'law of the Medes and Persians' was soon flatly and universally broken! We see this, for instance, in the book of Esther.

Chapter Seven

In chapter 5, we had the record of the last year, indeed of the last hours, of the kingship of Belshazzar. As we open chapter 7, we are carried back to the first year of his reign. At this time Daniel had sunk into complete obscurity, as chapter 5 bears witness. He had lost touch with worldly fame, but by a dream he was still in touch with heaven. Previously his fame had largely rested upon his God-given interpretations of dreams, though in chapter 2 the interpretation was revealed to him in 'a night vision'. Now, in his retirement from worldly affairs, by a dream a prophetic revelation is given to him, and 'he wrote the dream', for our benefit, since it has been included in the inspired Scriptures.

Verse 2 is very instructive. What he saw was produced by the striving of 'the four winds of the heaven ... upon the great sea'. Now the sea is used figuratively as indicating the masses of mankind, as are the 'many waters' of Revelation 17:1 and 15, which represent 'peoples, and multitudes, and nations'. So also, 'wind' often represents the power of Satan, for he is 'the prince of the power of the air' (Ephesians 2:2). What Daniel saw was, in figure, the forces of darkness working on the masses of mankind, and as a result producing, as we shall see, the four world-empires that fill up the times of the Gentiles. Israel is the only nation that has been raised up by God to a place of supremacy; but, while it is set aside, four world-powers arise as a result of the striving of Satanic forces, and not of the working of God's power.

The powers that emerge are represented by 'beasts'. It is worthy of note that this figure re-appears in the book of Revelation, where the revival of the Roman Empire in the last days is presented as 'a beast' rising up 'out of the sea' (13:1). That the four empires should be portrayed as beasts is no compliment to them. But God does not pay compliments, but pre-figures things exactly as they are, according to their inward nature. History, as far as it has been enacted up to the present, quite supports the accuracy of the figure used.

The four beasts appear in rotation, and are described in verses 4-7. The first was the Babylonian, with the strength of a lion and the swiftness of an eagle, and the latter part of verse 4 seems to refer to God's disciplinary dealings with Nebuchadnezzar. This had been nearly fulfilled when Daniel had the dream.

The second, described in verse 5, was the Medo-Persian, that overthrew the Babylonian soon after Daniel had the dream. It is represented as a bear, which is worthy of note. The Babylonian was like a lion and an eagle, as we see also in Jeremiah 4:7, and 49:19-22. Now the bear in nature has not the strength of the lion, but it is marked by rapacity, as indicated in our verse. History records that 'one side' of it, namely the Median, came up first, for Darius was a Mede; but soon Cyrus the Persian became dominant. He became favourable to the Jews, as the opening verses of Ezra show, but apart from this its power was not tolerant, and the words, 'Arise, devour much flesh', were fulfilled in its history.

In verse 6, the third empire is prefigured, which we know as the Grecian, founded by Alexander the Great. Now a leopard is a cruel beast, marked by great agility. The idea of swift agility is increased by this beast having 'four wings of a fowl' on its back. This aptly sets forth the swiftness of Alexander's conquests, and his overthrow of the Persian empire. It also had 'four heads', and in this we see an allusion to what followed the early death of Alexander—the division of the empire into four separate states, under four of his leading generals.

But a fourth empire was to arise, as stated in verse 7; namely the Roman, which would be so remarkable that no well-known beast, such as lion, bear or leopard, could represent it. It would be, 'diverse from all the beasts that were before it', — 'dreadful and terrible, and strong exceedingly'. Its teeth would be 'iron', and it would not only subdue, but also devour and break in pieces all that it subdued. How exactly this described the Roman empire, history bears witness.

Here then we have the four world-empires, that were indicated in Nebuchadnezzar's dream, recorded in chapter 2. But they are presented in a very different aspect. There the deterioration in the quality of their governments, descending from gold to an unreliable combination of iron and clay, was indicated. Here we have their true inner character and spirit set before us; and all four are beasts, endowed with great strength, which is used with destructive force. What a terrible unveiling is here before us as to the true character, as God sees it, of the mighty empires of men, which are to fill up the times of the Gentiles. Let us ponder these things deeply, and learn to view world affairs in the light of what is here made known to us.

The fourth beast had ten horns, answering to the ten toes at the base of the image, in chapter 2. Verses 8 and 9 of our chapter show that these 'horns' prefigure powerful men and kings, that will arise in the last days of the fourth beast. Of these, three will be overthrown before 'another little horn', to be marked by penetrating intelligence and great powers of boastful speech. Here, for the first time, we meet with that evil man in whom Satan's power will be personified, as we shall see lower down in our chapter.

As Daniel gazed at this remarkable sight, 'thrones were set, and the Ancient of days did sit' (New Trans.); that is, he saw the hour of God's judgment arrived. How majestic is the language of these verses! One cannot read them without being reminded of the way the Lord Jesus appeared to John, as he records in Revelation 1. We remember also that 'the Father judgeth no man, but hath committed all judgment unto the Son' (John 5:22). To Pharisees and others John the Baptist declared, 'He shall baptize you with the Holy Ghost, and with fire …

He will burn up the chaff with unquenchable fire' (Matthew 3:11-12); and 'fire', you notice, marks the scene we have before us here.

The 'Ancient of days' then presents God to us in the eternity of His Being, for we must remember that the Persons of the Godhead were not clearly distinguished, as they have been since the coming of Christ. In the presence of Almighty God the Roman empire in its last and worst phase, under the domination of the 'little horn', whom we identify with the first beast of Revelation 13, will be destroyed in judgment; while up to that time the three earlier beasts will have been permitted to exist, though dominion had been taken from them, as stated in verse 12.

This dream clearly divides into three parts. The first, the vision of the four beasts. The second, the vision of judgment established and the fourth beast with its little horn destroyed in the presence of Almighty God. The third, the vision of the advent and glory and eternal dominion of 'the Son of Man'. The allusion to the Lord Jesus here is not as distinct as it is in Psalm 8:4, where the first 'man' represents the Hebrew word meaning 'mortal man', and the second is the word 'Adam'. He was not mortal man, but He was indeed 'Son of Adam', as Luke's Gospel shows. In verse 13, however, it is really, 'a son of man' (New Trans.), and the word in the Chaldee is the one used for mortal man. Daniel saw the One in the vision as being *like* a son of man, and this He was, for He was 'made in the *likeness* of men' (Philippians 2:7). In the light of the New Testament we are privileged to know who He really is.

From verse 15 to the end of the chapter we have the explanation that was given to Daniel, of the vision he had seen. Much of it we have already mentioned, but there are in it details not represented in the dream. In verses 18 and 25, for instance, we find mentioned 'the saints of the most High', or 'of the high places'. When the fourth beast is destroyed, together with the 'horn', which is its imperial head, these saints will take the kingdom and possess it for ever. Yet some of them will be worn out, or destroyed. As verse 21 says, the 'horn' made war with the saints, 'and prevailed against them'.

We have here a brief allusion to things more clearly revealed in Revelation 13:7 and 14:9-13. We ask our readers to read these verses, noting particularly the 13th verse, and then turning to verse 4 of chapter 20. It seems plain then that the 'horn' who is the first 'beast' of Revelation 13, will persecute and slay many of the godly, who refuse him and his 'mark'. But such will be blessed in a particular degree, as resting from their labours, and they will be raised before the start of Christ's reign, to share in a heavenly portion and have dominion given to them, in common with all others, who are 'of the high places'; that is, enjoying a *heavenly* portion, as distinct from a place in millennial blessedness *on earth*.

Not all the saints, mentioned in verse 21 of our chapter, are slain, though war is made against them. These of course will pass into the earthly blessedness of the Kingdom. So, in our chapter we have 'the saints', who will escape and be blessed on earth: 'the saints of the high places', whose portion is in heaven: and further, in verse 27, 'the *people of* the saints of the high places', to whom the greatness of the kingdom '*under the whole heaven*', is to be given. That people will be the true Israel, cleansed and born again, as predicted in Ezekiel 36, and thus made spiritually to live, according to Ezekiel 37.

This vision was given to Daniel shortly before the first of the four great empires fell, and since he was without the further light shed in the New Testament, we can understand what a disturbing effect it had on his mind. What *disturbed* him may well *encourage* us. The beast-like empires of men will vanish in judgment, and all dominion will be vested in the Son of Man, while delegated authority will be exercised by saints both heavenly and earthly.

CHAPTER EIGHT

We now leave that portion of the prophecy that deals specially with the Gentile powers; and so, as we begin chapter 8, the language of the original reverts to Hebrew from the Chaldee. The vision recorded in this chapter, is dated about two years after the one we have just considered. Though Gentile powers are still in view, the main point seems to be their action in regard to Jerusalem with its sanctuary and sacrifices. It came to Daniel not when he was in Babylon but rather in Shushan; that is, in a palace of the Medo-Persian empire, which overthrew the Babylonian, and it must have been just before that overthrow took place.

Thus before the Medo-Persian empire triumphed, its own overthrow was pictured in the mind of Daniel, since the ram with two horns clearly represented that power. The Persian horn became the dominant one, but it came up last. For a time the ram was irresistible, doing its own will and pushing in all directions.

The he goat of verse 5 is clearly the Grecian power, and the 'notable horn' was a prediction of Alexander the Great, who, moving with great swiftness, crushed the Persian power. Then verse 8 predicted the sudden end of Alexander and the division of his newly acquired dominion into four lesser ones.

Thus far, we have been given an enlarged view of what was compressed into verse 6 of the previous chapter; but in verse 9 of chapter 8 we pass into predictions that are new, and that deal with happenings that would spring out of the dissolution of the Grecian empire rather than the affairs of the last days, until we come to the interpretation of the vision, which is given to us in verses 19-26. As is frequently the case, the interpretation travels beyond the details given in the vision.

The predictions, as to 'the little horn' and his doings, are distinct from those of the 'little horn', of chapter 7. That was to spring out of the fourth empire in its last days: this, out of one of the four parts of the divided third empire. This striking individual was to glorify himself and reach towards the south and east and 'the pleasant land', which doubtless is Palestine. The 'stars' he would cast down, we understand to be shining servants of God. He would take away the daily sacrifice and tread the sanctuary down, dishonouring the 'prince of the host'. This was all fulfilled in the career of that evil man, known to history as Antiochus Epiphanes. He defiled the temple and tried to force heathen worship on the Jews, which led to the revolt under the Maccabees, and a time of much tribulation, until at last after the 2,300 evenings and mornings the sanctuary was cleansed. We believe that many details given in Hebrews 11:35-38, may refer to saints of those days.

When Daniel was made to understand the vision, his thoughts were soon carried on to 'what shall be in the last end of the indignation', as verse 19 says. Verses 20-22, summarize the history we have considered, and then verse 23 carries us on to the latter days, when two things will happen. First, transgressors will have 'come to the full'. Second, a king, marked by bold power and clever understanding, will rise up from the same quarter. This is indicated by the fact that he arises in the latter time of 'their kingdom'; that is, from the north region of Syria, whence came Antiochus of evil memory, who sprang from Seleucus, one of Alexander's generals, who became king of the north, while Ptolemy and his successors became kings of the south, or Egypt.

This coming king of the north, like Antiochus, will attempt to 'destroy the mighty and the holy people'; that is, the Israel of the last days. His doings are described in verses 24 and 25, but at the last he will 'stand up against the Prince of princes', and as a result be broken 'without hand'; that is, we understand, without human instrumentality. Here then, we have that 'king of the north', or 'the Assyrian', that figures so largely in other Old Testament prophecies, who will be destroyed by the Lord Jesus Himself when He appears in His glory, and His feet stand on the Mount of Olives, as Zechariah has predicted in the opening of his 14th chapter.

It is important, we believe, to keep clear in our minds the distinction between this 'little horn', proceeding from the third beast, and the one on the fourth beast in chapter 7, who is supported by the false Messiah in Jerusalem, according to Revelation 13; and that means of course that he is in league with the Jew and Jerusalem, whereas this northern king is violently against them. Both, though probably not at the same moment, will be destroyed by the glorious appearing of Christ.

DANIEL

Daniel was assured that this vision was true and certain, though what it portrayed was distant from his days. Though the terror of it caused him to faint, he understood it not. It was to be as a sealed book in his day. It is an open vision to us, since we have the light of the New Testament and are indwelt by the Spirit of God. We may well exclaim, 'Thanks be unto God for His unspeakable gift'!

CHAPTER NINE

What is recorded in chapter 9 took place shortly after Darius had overthrown Babylon and taken the kingdom—that is, soon after the experience Daniel had, as narrated in chapter 5. By this time he was of course an old man, and near the end of his life of service, for he had been amongst the first batch of captives, deported by Nebuchadnezzar. Jeremiah, an older man, had been left in Jerusalem, prophesying there until its destruction years later.

The fall of Babylon was a tremendous upheaval. What effect had it upon Daniel? It moved him to study that portion of the Word of God that was available under his hand. A first-rate example for us today, since the upheavals among the nations during the past fifty years have been more far-reaching than the fall of Babylon. The prophecies of Jeremiah had been committed to writing and were available to him as, 'books'. We have the completed Bible, which really means 'The Book'.

To Daniel these 'books' came as 'the word of the Lord'; that is, he received Jeremiah's writings as being inspired of God, and hence authoritative, and to be accepted without question. Happy are we if, following his example, we treat our Bible in the same way. The particular passage that affected Daniel so deeply was Jeremiah 25:8-14, where 'desolations' lasting 70 years were predicted. Daniel must at once have realized that the 70 years had nearly run their course, and that deliverance of some kind was near at hand. The effect that this discovery had upon him is most instructive and also searching for us.

Had we been in his place we might have felt greatly exhilarated by the discovery, and inclined to have a time of jubilation. But it was not thus with Daniel; but rather the exact opposite. He was moved to fasting, humiliation, confession and prayer, realizing the great sin of his people which had brought all this judgment upon them. This we see, if verses 4-19 of our chapter be read. He utterly condemned himself as identified with his people, and he vindicated God in His judgments, proclaiming His righteousness in all He had done.

These words of Daniel should be deeply pondered by each of us. Nowhere in the Bible do we find a finer example of thorough-going confession and prayer, though Ezra's prayer recorded in chapter 9 of his book closely resembles it. He made no allusion to the covenant of promise made with Abraham, but placed himself before God on the basis of the covenant of the law of Moses, and the subsequent ministry through the prophets. As to this he confessed complete breakdown and disaster, though personally he was less implicated in it than any in his day.

But thus it always is. Those deeply implicated in failure and sin are by that very fact rendered insensible to the depths into which they have sunk, while those less involved are painfully alive to the state of things. What is the state of things in the professing church today? A prophetic sketch of church history is given us in Revelation 2 and 3. The last stage is that of Laodicea. Are those deeply involved in its grievous evils likely to bow down in confession and prayer? **No.** Only those who are lightly involved will do so. May we all take heed to this.

The things that mark true confession come clearly to light here. The evil is acknowledged without any attempt at excuse or extenuation. The rightness of God's judgments and discipline are fully acknowledged, and the plea that God would grant deliverance, according to His word, is urged, 'not … for our righteousnesses, but for Thy great mercies'. Let us cultivate these excellent features in our day. We too can ask for nothing on the ground of *merit*, but only on the ground of *mercy*. As we contemplate the state of Christendom today, and of our own state too, let us cultivate the spirit of humble confession that marked Daniel.

Such confession and prayer meets with an immediate answer, as we see in verses 20 and 21. Gabriel, the angelic messenger of God, was sent, 'to fly swiftly', with an answer that would give Daniel 'skill and understanding' as to events that lay ahead, with the assurance that he was in God's estimation a man 'greatly beloved'. What other saint was permitted to hear himself so described? Our Lord's words were, 'he that shall humble himself shall be exalted' (Matthew 23:12). Here we have an illustration of this. Daniel had humbled himself in exceptional measure, and so he is permitted to know that he is greatly beloved in Heaven. What an exaltation! Had he not been truly humbled such an assurance might have puffed him up to his undoing.

Gabriel was commissioned to reveal to Daniel the prophecy of the 'seventy weeks'; the word week here indicating a period of seven, it may be of days, or as here it clearly is, of years. We have just seen Daniel stirred to confession and prayer by the discovery of the fact that the seventy years of the desolations had nearly run their course; he is now to learn that seventy years, multiplied by seven, were to pass when according to the Divine reckoning, full release and blessing would be reached, as indicated in verse 24.

The contents of this verse must be carefully noted. In the first place, the time indicated is determined upon 'thy people and upon thy holy city', and not upon the world in general; though doubtless what transpires upon Israel and Jerusalem will have great effect upon the world in general. Then, in the second place, the end that is to be reached is the establishment of full millennial blessedness. Then it is that the sad story of transgression and sin will be closed; then 'the righteousness of the ages' (New Trans.) will be brought in; then the vision and the prophecy will be sealed up, since all is accomplished: then 'the most holy' or, 'the holy of holies' will be anointed, and set apart for God, as is also predicted in such a passage as Ezekiel 43:12. The end of the seventy years of desolations would only be a very faint and imperfect forecast of this.

The seventy weeks, or 490 years, were, however, to be divided into three parts, and they were to start when the commandment was issued to restore and to build Jerusalem as a city. The opening verses of Ezra give us the edict of Cyrus to rebuild the *temple*: the edict to rebuild the *city* was that of Artaxerxes, as recorded in Nehemiah 2. This latter was the start of the seventy weeks, predicted here. The first part—seven weeks, or

49 years—were to be occupied with the rebuilding, and the re-establishment of Israel in the city and land: that is, about up to the time of Malachi. Then were to come the 62 weeks, or 434 years, completing the period 'unto the Messiah the Prince'.

Here then we have a very clear and definite prophecy, which has been fulfilled. In checking its fulfilment the main difficulty lies in the fact that the Jews calculated their years in a way different from ourselves, which gives rise to complications. We are content to accept the result of an investigation made years ago by the late Sir Robert Anderson, a competent and reliable person. He showed that not only were the 483 years to Christ correct, but that they expired exactly to the day on which He made His formal presentation of Himself to His people, riding on the foal of an ass, as Zechariah had foretold.

And what was the result of this presentation? Just what we have in verse 26. Messiah was 'cut off, but not for Himself', or better, as the margin has it, 'and shall have nothing'. Thus His rejection was foretold, and though He had the title to *everything* on the earth, He had *nothing*: a borrowed stable for His birth; nowhere to lay His head, while He served; a borrowed tomb at the finish. Here then we find the Jews committing themselves to a sin far worse than their breaking of the law and their persistent idolatry. The consequences flowing from this greatest of all sins, are stated at the end of verse 26.

Years ago we heard of a Christian talking to a Jewish Rabbi, and asking him what in their history justified God in condemning them to the disasters and miseries they suffered in Babylon. He admitted at once that it was their law-breaking and idolatry. Then, said the Christian, tell me, what have you done that justifies God in condemning you to far worse disasters and miseries, lasting from A.D. 70, to the present time, with even worse things still in prospect? It was a devastating question, and what could he say? We know what we should at once say; pointing to the Messiah crucified between two thieves.

In this prophecy the result of the cutting off of the Messiah is briefly summed up at the end of verse 26. The more immediate result was to be the destruction of the city and the sanctuary by 'the *people* of the prince that shall come'. Now this prince is the 'little horn', of whom we read in chapter 7, the head of the Roman Empire in its revived and last stage, whom we identified with the first 'beast' of Revelation 13. This Roman despot is still to come, but the Roman *people* were the dominant power in the time of our Lord, and they did destroy Jerusalem in very thorough fashion.

That destruction was but the beginning of God's disciplinary judgments upon them. So the prophecy moves on to 'the end thereof', which is to be 'with a flood', or 'an overflow', indicating, we judge, that the sorrows and persecutions that have followed the Jews through all these centuries will rise to flood-tide height just before the end. The closing words of this verse may be read, 'unto the end, war, —the desolations determined'. Here is a statement conveying volumes in a few words.

In the past nineteen centuries war has been the prominent feature. If all reference to it were cut out of our history books, there would be not much history left, and there are wars predicted, that yet have to come. But the Jew and his city are particularly in view in this prophecy, and hence we again meet with the word, 'desolations'. Our chapter began with a reference to the 70 years' desolations predicted by Jeremiah; now as we reach its end we find another prediction of desolations, which in length and final severity will surpass the former. So Messiah's death was to be followed almost immediately by the destruction of Jerusalem, and ultimately, for a long period, but its length not revealed, by war and desolations.

Having mentioned the end in verse 26, we are carried on to the events of the end in verse 27. Who is the 'he', with whom the verse begins? Clearly the 'prince that shall come', dominating the revived Roman Empire of the last days. He is going to confirm, not '*the* covenant' but, '*a* covenant with the many for one week' (New Trans.). And this is evidently the one week which completes the 70 weeks of this prophecy. This covenant, we judge, will permit the Jews of that day to resume 'the sacrifice and the oblation' in Jerusalem, for in the midst of the week he will break the covenant, and the desolations will reach their climax.

In the New Translation the close of the verse reads, 'because of the protection of abominations [there shall be] a desolator, even until that the consumption and what is determined shall be poured out upon the desolate'. This will be the time of the great tribulation, and the 'desolator' we should identify as being the 'king of fierce countenance', spoken of in the closing verses of chapter 8. At the end of this seventieth week Messiah will appear in power and great glory, as other scriptures show, and the 'everlasting righteousness', or 'the righteousness of the ages', will be established. His appearing will completely overthrow the desolator and completely deliver the desolate.

Thus, the day of grace, in which we are living, comes in between weeks 69 and 70. The latter part of verse 26 shows that there is to be an undefined period at that point, marked by war and desolations as to world affairs and the Jews, but marked also by the going forth of the Gospel, as the New Testament shows. The rejection and the death of the Messiah was thus plainly predicted, with the sorrows of the world in general and of the Jew in particular, as the result of it.

CHAPTER TEN

As we commence reading chapter 10, we again find mention of 'weeks'. They are, however, to be distinguished from the 'weeks' we have just been considering, since a note in the margin of our Bibles indicates that in the Hebrew they are 'weeks of days'. For those weeks Daniel was mourning and fasting, though the reason for this is not stated.

At the end of chapter 1, we were told that Daniel continued to the first year of Cyrus: what we are about to consider occurred in the third year of Cyrus, so Daniel was now an old man and very near the end of his remarkable career. Our chapter furnishes us with details preparatory to the prophetic revelations made in chapters 11 and 12. They are very instructive, as showing us the way in which angelic beings may act as 'ministering spirits, sent forth to minister for them who shall be heirs of salvation' (Hebrews 1:14).

Verses 5-9 describe the angelic visitation and the effect it had upon Daniel. We may remark that uniformly when angelic beings assume a form visible to human eyes, they appear as men. Nevertheless that which is supernatural marks them, reminding the one who sees them of the presence of God. It was so on this occasion, and the description given in verse 6 reminds us of John's description of his Lord, as recorded in Revelation 1:14-15. Yet the angel here was not the Lord, as verse 13, we think, makes plain. Still it put Daniel on his face and prostrate.

There is also a resemblance between this scene and what took place at the conversion of Saul of Tarsus. Then his companions saw the light but did not hear the words that were spoken though they heard the sound. Here the men with him saw nothing but they were filled with trembling, and fled to hide themselves. Fallen man cannot stand in the presence of God, and even a saint— whether Daniel in the Old Testament or John in the New—falls down 'in a deep sleep', or 'as one dead'. We know God as our Father, but we must never forget His supreme majesty as God.

In the first year of Darius, Daniel was addressed as a man 'greatly beloved', as we saw in the last chapter. We have now come to the third year of Cyrus, and again he is thus addressed twice, showing he had not forfeited the earlier description. And why was this, seeing that so often saints backslide, and do not maintain the life of godliness? The answer, we think, is found in verse 12. In his devoted life Daniel had maintained two things.

In the first place he had set his heart to understand. How often is this lacking amongst us today! Is it our fervent desire to understand what God has revealed, not with the head only, but with the heart? Daniel loved his God, and loved his people, so that what God made known deeply affected him. If love were more fervent with us, we should be setting our *hearts* to understand the truth made known to us.

In the second place he 'chastened', or 'humbled' himself before God, while he sought the understanding. Here again we have to challenge ourselves. It is fatally easy to desire a large understanding of Divine truth because it confers a certain prominence and importance upon the person who possesses it. In reality all truth, if apprehended in the heart, *humbles* us. This is exemplified in the Apostle Paul. Writing of God's great thoughts as to the church in Ephesians 3, he is '*less* than the *least* of all saints'. In 2 Corinthians 12, after telling how he had been caught up into Paradise, and heard unspeakable things, he says, 'though I be *nothing*'. Did we chasten ourselves more truly before God, we should soon have a larger understanding of His truth.

Verses 12 and 13 show that answers to our prayerful desires may be delayed by adverse powers in the unseen world. Satan has his angels, and it appears that some may be deputed by him to hinder God's work in certain kingdoms. The prince of the kingdom of Persia, who withstood the holy angel speaking to Daniel, was doubtless a fallen angelic being. Michael, elsewhere called the archangel, came to help him. The first verse of chapter 12 shows us that Michael is specially commissioned to act on behalf of the children of Israel, and hence he intervened on this occasion. In the last verse of our chapter he is called, 'your prince'.

In the angelic world there was also 'the prince of Grecia', as verse 20 shows; but in spite of these adverse powers the messenger of God had come to Daniel, and lifting him up had strengthened him to receive the communication that God was now sending him.

Conflict in the angelic realm had still to take place with the princes of Persia and Grecia—the empire that was presently to overthrow the Persian empire—but the instruction of this humble and devoted servant of God took precedence, as to time, over even that.

He had come to show Daniel, 'that which is noted in the Scripture of Truth'. He spoke as if it had already been so noted, but we may indeed thank God that it has been noted in the Bible—the Scripture of Truth—which we hold in our hand and can read today. What was thus conveyed to Daniel is noted in the chapters that follow, and as we read them we shall see that some things revealed have already taken place, and some remain to be fulfilled, as we have just seen in the prophecy of the seventy weeks. What has been so accurately fulfilled assures us that the important things, that remain to be fulfilled, will all take place with equal accuracy in their season.

CHAPTER ELEVEN

We now come to the last of the prophetic revelations, received and recorded by Daniel. The opening verses of chapter 11, indeed the larger part of the chapter, give us predictions that very evidently have long since been fulfilled. If our readers will glance at the close of verse 35, they will see the words, 'to the time of the end, because it is yet for a time appointed'. Then turning back to chapter 9:26, they will see the words, 'unto the end'; and at that point came the undisclosed gap in the prophecy of the seventy weeks—as we now know, lasting over nineteen centuries—before the seventieth week arrives. So it is, we believe, here, and only when we reach verse 36 of our chapter does the prophecy suddenly move on to the time of the end, and to the last days.

The three Persian kings who were to 'stand up', according to verse 2, are evidently the three mentioned in Ezra 4:5-7, known in history as Cambyses, Smerdis, and Darius Hystaspes. The fourth, 'richer than they all', would be Xerxes, who was so intoxicated by his own greatness that he attacked Greece, and stirred up the 'mighty king' of verse 3—Alexander the Great—to humble his pride and shatter his kingdom; gaining for himself 'great dominion', according to his own will.

History records how brief was Alexander's dominion, for he died when still young, and his kingdom was divided between four of his generals, as is clearly foretold in verse 4. Their powers, however, were far more limited and 'not according to his dominion'. From verse 5 onward, our attention is directed to the doings of two out of these four; the king of the south and the king of the north respectively. If we enquire why the prophecy concentrates on these two only, the answer surely is that only these two meddled with and oppressed the Jews back in the land. Their kingdoms were north and south of Palestine; what we should now call Syria and Egypt, and the first kings were Seleucus and Ptolemy.

The New Translation renders verse 5 as, 'The king of the south, who is one of his princes, shall be strong; but [another] shall be stronger than he'. Both of these princes of Alexander would be strong, but the northern one the stronger of the two. This exactly came to pass.

Verse 6 begins 'And in the end of years', and we at once travel on some distance into history, for the prophecy does not concern itself here with individual kings. It is just 'the king of the north', or 'of the south', though different individuals may be indicated. What is plainly foretold is the state of friction and warfare that continued for many years between these two opposing powers, to the trouble and discomfort of the Palestinian Jews, who were located between them. We may say therefore that verses 6-20 forecast their evil schemings and fightings up to a point when the power of Rome became manifest, before which the then king of the north should 'stumble and fall, and not be found'. His successor had to be a mere 'raiser of taxes', to meet the demands of Rome. Infidels have insisted this chapter must have been written after the events, so accurately does it foretell what actually took place.

Reaching verse 21, we read that after this 'raiser of taxes' there would 'stand up a vile person', marked equally by cunning flattery and by warlike violence, and his doings and the things that sprang out of his doings occupy us until we come to the end of verse 36. We have here again, we believe, the man presented to us in chapter 8:9, as the 'little horn' rising out of one of the four kingdoms into which the Grecian dominion was divided—the man known to history as Antiochus Epiphanes. His evil doings are dwelt upon at some length, we believe, because he acted with such violence against the Jews as to make him a type or forecast of the king of the north, who in the last days will be their great adversary.

This is seen especially in verses 28-32. In the first of these verses, 'his heart shall be against the holy covenant'. Then for a time his plans are spoiled by 'the ships of Chittim'; that is, an expedition from Rome. This was the occasion that some of us may remember hearing about in our school days, when tired with his falsity the Roman leader drew a circle about him where he stood, and demanded an answer before he stepped out of it. This it was that angered him, and as he dared not attack the Romans, he vented his spleen on the Jews, and had 'indignation against the holy covenant'.

Amongst the Jews of his days were found some 'that forsake the holy covenant', as verse 30 indicates, and establishing contact with these, he proceeded to pollute the sanctuary in a violent way, as verse 31 predicts. He overturned the whole order of things in the temple at Jerusalem, stopping the sacrifices to Jehovah in the endeavour to make all venerate a false image, which is described here as 'the abomination that maketh desolate'. Then he corrupted and gained to his side by flatteries 'such as do wickedly against the covenant'.

Let us notice that no less than four times the 'covenant' is mentioned in these verses, and on three of these occasions the word 'holy' is connected with it. What God has covenanted and decreed is always the object of the devil's attack, and this man was without a doubt an agent of Satan in his efforts to subvert what remained of the worship of the one true God at Jerusalem.

But in those days there were to be found not only those who were wicked and whom he could corrupt but also 'people that do know their God', and, 'that understand among the people'. This is ever God's way. He does not leave Himself without a witness of some kind, and here we have a prediction of what actually happened in those dark days. The Maccabees were raised up, zealous and God-fearing men, and under their leadership there was ultimately a deliverance, though not without much loss and suffering, as is indicated in verse 33.

In the closing verses of Hebrews 11, particularly in verses 36-38, we find allusions to the sufferings of saints of a bygone age which we can hardly identify from Old Testament history, and it may be that the reference is to saints who suffered in this period of trial, after the days of Malachi. Their testings were intensified by the failure and apostasy of some who were men of understanding, as verse 35 of our chapter predicted; but this would have a purging effect upon those who did really stand firmly for God.

This mixed state of things is to persist, 'to the time of the end'. Thus it is stated, and thus it has been—particularly as regards the Jew, who is before us in the prophecy here. There is to be in this matter 'a time appointed', but no indication is given of how long the time is to be. We turn to such New Testament passages as Ephesians 3:4-5, and Colossians 1:25-26, to find that in our epoch of Gospel grace going out to the Gentiles, God is working out designs that He had from eternity, but which were not revealed in Old Testament times. In the wisdom of God, however, the prophecies were so worded as to leave room for the things subsequently to be made known without any collision of fact. An illustration of this, often referred to, is in Isaiah 61:2, where both Advents are alluded to in one verse. The same thing may be said of chapter 9:26 of our book, and of the verse before us here.

In verse 36, 'the king' is suddenly introduced to us, and glancing at verse 40 we discover that his dominion will be 'at the time of the end', and also that his kingdom will be found in a land lying between the kings of the south and the north. We conclude therefore that he is a king who will dominate Palestine in the last days, and of whom we read further in the New Testament. He is to be identified, we believe, with the second beast of Revelation 13, and with that false Messiah, coming 'in his own name', whom the Lord Jesus predicted in John 5:43.

The doings of this 'king' are predicted in verses 36-39, and the leading feature is this: —he 'shall do according to his will'. Now sin is lawlessness—the creature breaking loose from the control of the Creator, in order to assert and accomplish its own will. In 2 Thessalonians 2:3, we read of 'that man of sin', who is to be revealed when He who restrains is removed, and if that passage be compared with this, we at once see some striking resemblances, for in both the leading features of this coming great one are self-will and self-exaltation.

Let us each remember for our own soul's good that there is nothing more destructive of true Christian life than self-will. We are called to do, not our own wills but the will of God. We are called to a life of obedience, for we are to have in us the mind that was in Christ, which led Him even to death. His was the life of self-humiliation, the exact opposite to the self-exalting mind which was in Adam, and which characterizes the flesh in each one of us.

Two expressions in verse 37 indicate that this king will be a Jew, for he disregards 'the God of his fathers', and also 'the desire of women', for every typical Jewish woman desired to be the mother of the Messiah. He will speak 'marvellous things' against the true God, assuming a God-like position for himself. Yet he will honour 'the god of forces', or 'of fortresses'; an allusion we think, to what is plainly seen in Revelation 13, where the second beast is the leader in religious apostasy but is dependent upon the first beast for worldly power and military might.

Support he will need, for the kings of both south and north will be antagonistic, more particularly the king of the north, as we see in the closing verses of the chapter. In Isaiah he is spoken of as the Assyrian, and 'the overflowing scourge' (28:15), and Zechariah 14:1-3 appears to refer to the end of this northern adversary, as predicted in the two verses that close our chapter. At the outset he will have great success, overflowing many lands, save Edom, Moab and Ammon, who are reserved to be dealt with more directly by a restored Israel. He will even overpower Egypt, and then tidings from the north-east will lead him to Palestine, and he will 'plant the tents of his palace between the sea and the mountain of holy beauty' (New Trans.). And then, when his achievements seem to reach their climax, 'he shall come to his end, and none shall help him'. In this terse yet graphic way was revealed to Daniel what is stated in Zechariah 14:3. Jehovah goes forth to the conflict, in the person of the Lord Jesus. The adverse northern king is crushed, and comes to his end.

CHAPTER TWELVE

There will be, however, other antagonistic powers beside the kings of north and south and the false Messiah-king in Jerusalem. All will be dealt with for 'at that time', as the opening verse of chapter 12 declares, God is going to resume His dealings with Israel in His grace. Michael the archangel is specially commissioned to act on their behalf, and he stands up to deal with things, and two great events come to pass. First, there will be a complete deliverance to Daniel's people.

This time of great trouble is evidently the time our Lord referred to in His prophetic discourse as the 'great tribulation' (Matthew 24:21), after He had spoken of 'the abomination of desolation, spoken of by Daniel the prophet'. In this He referred to verse 11 of this twelfth chapter, and not to verse 31 of chapter 11, which though something of the same kind clearly refers to what took place under Antiochus Epiphanes. This verse in Daniel 12 is the first definite prophecy of this fearful time of tribulation which lies ahead.

And it is worthy of note that this first prediction clearly relates it to the Jew, as also does the Lord's prophecy, recorded in Matthew 24 and Mark 13. It will be the climax of God's governmental dealings with that people, who rejected and crucified their Messiah, though as Revelation 3:10 indicates, all the world will be affected by it, since the Gentiles as a secondary power had a hand in the death of Christ. In that tribulation there will be not only terrible evils, proceeding from both man and Satan, but the outpouring of the wrath of God, as revealed in Revelation 16. As Christians we have the assurance that, 'God hath not appointed us to wrath, but to obtain salvation by our Lord Jesus Christ' (1 Thessalonians 5:9).

Our scripture tells us that an elect Israel will be delivered out of the tribulation— 'every one that shall be found written in the book'; the book of life, as the New Testament speaks of it. The awakening that is predicted in verse 2, is evidently similar to that of which Ezekiel 37 speaks. Many a Jew will be asleep as regards their God, and buried in the dust of the nations. They will awake, some marked by faith to enter into the life everlasting of the millennial age; others still unbelieving to enter into judgment. It will be with them as it will be with Gentile peoples, as the Lord made known in Matthew 25:31-46.

It will also be, as verse 3 shows, a time of reward for the wise and diligent in the service of their God. Let us all take good note of this, for the principles on which God deals with His servants do not vary. There is reward for the 'wise', those who have a God-given understanding of His truth and ways, so as to instruct others also; and a reward also for those who are active in the winning of souls, so as to turn them into the way of righteousness. Thus what we may call the contemplative side of Christian life and the active side of service are to be equally balanced.

Verse 4 closes the prophetic communication that began with chapter 11, and it corroborates the statement that from verse 36 onwards we have revealed things that will come to pass at 'the time of the end'. Though made known to Daniel and recorded by him, it was to be as a shut book till the end time was reached. During the last century or so these things have been much studied and the light of them has shone forth. This should confirm us in the thought that the end of the age is near.

And the closing words of this verse should confirm us even further: 'many shall run to and fro, and knowledge shall be increased.' Our age is strikingly marked by both these things. Our powers of locomotion have increased beyond the dreams of our forebears—on land and sea, and in the air. But it is all to and from. We fly thither, and then back we come to our starting point, and end where we began. The increase of knowledge also is prodigious, even alarming in the field of nuclear energy, as everybody knows. Knowledge—Yes: but, wisdom—

No. Man is just the same sinful creature as of old—deceived by the adversary.

When we consider the dealings of God, particularly in judgment, the question that always arises in our minds is—How long? That was the enquiry between these angelic beings—appearing as men—that had conveyed the prophecy to Daniel. The answer is given in verse 7, and it plainly shows that the question was how long to the end of the time of trouble once it had begun? The answer was, 'a time, times, and an half', which we understand to signify, 3½ years; doubtless the second half of the seventieth week, indicated in chapter 9. When that last week is finished all power will have departed from 'the holy people'; that is, the God-fearing remnant in Israel. They will be marked by an extremity of weakness, and the adversaries will have reached apparently the peak of their power and splendour. Then the sudden appearing of the Lord in glory and might: His poor saints delivered; the adversaries irretrievably crushed.

Thus it has ever been, and thus it will yet be: Israel in Egypt, for instance. When Jacob went into Egypt in the days of Joseph he and his children were an honoured people. The years passed and they fell lower and lower, until they were a crowd of slaves under the task-master's lash. Then God acted in judgment: His powerless people delivered: the powerful enemy completely overthrown. Thus it will be for Israel at the opening of the millennial age; and we do not anticipate it will be otherwise when the saints are raptured to glory, as predicted in 1 Thessalonians 4. They will not have reached such a state of spiritual opulence that the angels might be tempted to think that they deserved it, but the very reverse. It will be the crowning act, not of merit, but of mercy, as we see in Jude 21.

Daniel's question, in verse 8, finds an echo in all our hearts. It now concerns not the time of the end, but what is to be the final outcome of all this human wickedness and of the dealings of God? Daniel was a godly Jew of a representative sort, and to such at that time the real significance was 'closed up and sealed'. We are told in 1 Peter 1:12 how Old Testament prophets spoke of things, which they themselves did not understand, as in their day redemption had not been accomplished, nor had the Holy Spirit been given. What Daniel was to know was that God would still maintain a people for Himself, who would be purified and made white and 'tried', or, 'refined', by all His dealings, while the wicked would still pursue their evil way in darkness. Only the wise would have the capacity to understand. This solemn fact is stated very clearly in 1 Corinthians 2:14.

So Daniel had to go his way without any clear answer to his question. He was given, however, supplementary information as to the closing periods, for in verses 11 and 12 we have mentioned the two periods of 1290 and 1335 days. According to Jewish reckoning a year consisted of 360 days, and therefore the 'time, times, and a half', of verse 7, would consist of 1260 days, and the 1290 days would mean one month beyond that, just as the 1335 days would be a month and a half further beyond. What Daniel could know was that he who waited in patience to the expiration of the longest period, was to enter into *blessing*.

So here in one word there is an answer to the question of verse 8. Daniel might not know any details but he could be assured that *blessing* lay at the end for the people of God. We have the same assurance only we have it in larger measure and fuller detail. However searching are God's judgments upon man's evil, for the humble and patient there is always blessing at the end. Another fact lies embedded in these words. God acts, whether in judgment or in blessing, in stages. He did so with Israel in Egypt. He did so again when the church was inaugurated. There was the forty days of His repeated manifestations in resurrection, followed by the ten days of waiting; and then the formation of the church by the shedding forth of the Holy Spirit.

So it will be in the last days, when the Kingdom of God arrives in manifested power, and the last word to Daniel is one of full assurance. Until it comes, rest is to be his portion, after a life of exceptional unrest and strain; and when it does come he has an appointed 'lot', in which he will stand—and we venture to think that his 'lot' will not be a small one.

And we too, each have our 'lot' at the end. As sharing in the place and portion of the church, we know how wonderful that will be. But, what about our 'lot' in the coming kingdom of our Lord? That will depend upon our faithfulness in service here. If in any measure our 'lot' in the kingdom is to be comparable with Daniel's, we must like him go through the present world in holy *separation* and *devotedness* to God.

Ezra

The closing vision, granted to the prophet Daniel, was given to him in the third year of Cyrus, king of Persia. If now we open our Bibles at the book of Ezra, we are carried back to the first year of that great monarch, whom the prophet Isaiah mentioned by name some two centuries before he ascended the throne. If we turn to Isaiah 44:28, we read the prediction of what he would do. Ezra 1:2 records his doing what Isaiah foretold.

The opening verse of the chapter refers to the prophecy of Jeremiah, which so stirred the spirit of Daniel, as he recorded in his ninth chapter. The prediction is found in Jeremiah 25:11-14. Daniel saw that its fulfilment must be near, and it moved him to the remarkable prayer that is recorded. Ezra has placed on record the exact way in which it was fulfilled.

The word 'Lord' in verse 2 is of course Jehovah, and Cyrus recognised Him as the 'God of Heaven', and not merely of the kingdoms of the earth. Nebuchadnezzar had been brought to a similar confession, as we saw in Daniel 4:37. As one reads the summary of the proclamation that Cyrus issued, recorded in verses 2 and 3, one cannot but think that he must have been informed of the prophecy, recorded in the opening verses of Isaiah 45, as well as the closing verse of the preceding chapter. It was no small thing that Cyrus should acknowledge the supreme glory and power of God in this striking way, and act in obedience to what God had commanded. It is not surprising that God should have spoken of him as, 'His anointed'.

The proclamation did not name any person or persons who were to go to Jerusalem and build the house, but rather threw the door open for any Jew to go whose heart stirred him up to do so, giving him the assurance that he was to be liberally helped in the project before him. Being thus worded it meant that those who responded would be in the main men of piety, whose hearts were alive to the glory of God and to the place of His Name, while the more worldly minded and selfish would be inclined to remain in their comfortable homes, established during the seventy years of captivity, and leave the task to others who were prepared to face the difficulties and privations.

It is to be noted that what Cyrus had in view was the building of 'the house of the Lord', and he was not concerned with the desolate state of the city. It was Nehemiah who, at a later date, became so concerned about the waste and desolate condition of Jerusalem that he obtained the permission of Artaxerxes to restore and to build the city. The decree granted to Nehemiah is the starting point of the prophecy of the 'seventy weeks', as noted in Daniel 9:25. It was a case of God's house, first; the city where men dwelt, second. This is a principle of abiding significance.

Yet the tendency to forget it is very strong. Those who answered to the proclamation of Cyrus soon forget it, as we discover when we read Haggai's prophecy. Very soon they were building their 'ceiled houses', while the house of God was lying 'waste'. The same tendency is strongly at work amongst the people of God today.

So let us carefully observe the analogy that exists between what happened in the history of Judaism and what has happened in the history of Christendom.

In Judaism the law given through Moses was largely ignored, and the kingly authority, established in David, so corrupted that the Babylonian captivity fell upon them. In Christendom the purity of the Gospel was soon lost, and the rule of the Spirit, through the Word, was perverted and corrupted into the carnal rule of men, called 'popes' in Rome, many of whom were leaders in iniquity. This corruption reached a climax in the fourteenth and fifteenth centuries. Now, just as a revival of an outward and geographical sort began under Cyrus—though a number of men of true piety were engaged in it—so in the sixteenth century God granted the beginning of a revival of a more inward and spiritual sort in the history of Christendom; and out of the spiritual 'Babylon', an emergence began, which has continued to our day. In the light of this, let us see what lessons we may learn from the opening chapters of the book of Ezra.

Verse 5 of the first chapter shows that there was a real work of God in the souls of many, including leaders both civil and religious, which led them to embrace at once the opportunity that was given for a return to the land of their fathers, to re-establish the worship of God by rebuilding His house. In the providence of God this was actively promoted by Cyrus, in addition to vessels of value, given by Jews who did not participate in the expedition to Jerusalem, he restored all the holy vessels of the house of the Lord, which Nebuchadnezzar had placed in the house of his gods. The *spiritual* work of God in the souls of His people was matched by a *providential* work of God in the surrounding world. Thus it has been again in more recent times.

CHAPTER TWO

Chapter 2, with the exception of the last three verses, is taken up with details as to the number of those who answered to the proclamation, named under the heads of their families. The heads are named and the families counted. God took note of them and put their names into His record, while those whose hearts did not stir them up to go are passed over in silence. Let us take note of this.

The first name mentioned is Zerubbabel, who became the 'Tirshatha', or civil Governor: the second, that of Jeshua, the priest called Joshua in the books of Haggai and Zechariah. These were the leaders in the migration of 42,360 people, besides some servants and other possessions. There was no re-establishment of the kingdom, as though the times of the Gentiles had ceased. They were still under Gentile suzerainty.

Still there was a definite revival; and the first mark of it was this: they got *back to God's original centre*. Compared with the total number of dispersed Jews they were but few, and many of the worldly sort may have nicknamed them 'Zerubbabelites', still they were not that, but simply a few who cared for their God, and sought His original centre.

In the second place, there was *no claim to powers they did not possess*, since they had been forfeited by previous failure, as we see in verses 59-63. Awkward questions arose, as to whether some were truly children of Israel, and whether others were really children of priests, their genealogies being lost. In earlier days these points might have been settled by an appeal to God through the 'Urim and with Thummim'. This had been lost and they were humble enough to acknowledge it. When God grants a revival after grievous failure, He may not be pleased to restore everything—especially as to outward manifestations of power—just as things were at the first. Let us take note of this—we again would say. Certain manifestations of power, that were seen in apostolic days, are not in evidence today.

A third mark of true revival is seen in *the spirit of devotion*, that marked some of the 'chief fathers' of the people, when back in the land, as recorded in the closing verses of chapter 2. This spirit may not have continued for long, but it was evidently there at the start. When God begins to work there is always a devoted response on the part of some of His people.

Chapter Three

As we begin to read the third chapter, a fourth feature of true revival is plainly manifested: *obedience to the Word of God*. In verse 2, and again in verse 4, we find the words, 'as it is written'. Their first recorded action, when back in their land, was to approach their God in the manner He had laid down at the first. There was a very great contrast between their present humble circumstances and the great days when the law was given and the tabernacle constructed under Moses, or the palmy days of Solomon, when the first temple was built, yet they recognized that what God may lay down at the start of His dispensations stands unchanged to the finish.

So they did not attempt innovations, according to their own ideas of what might be suitable, but just reverted to God's original Word. They began with the burnt offering, which lay at the basis of all God's dealings with them; and the seventh month being come, they observed the feast of tabernacles, which fell at that time. This they did though the foundation of the temple had not been laid. The burnt offerings very rightly preceded the 'house'. That, however, was not forgotten, as verse 7 shows. The necessary preparations for it were started, for it was the prime object of their return to the land.

Reaching verse 8, we pass on to the second year of their return and find them setting forward this work, so that the foundations of the house were actually laid. This provoked a very moving scene, in which both joy and sorrow were mingled. There was joyful praise and thanksgiving to God, according to the 'ordinance of David king of Israel', as was indeed fitting. In Psalm 136 it is stated of God twenty-six times that 'His mercy endureth for ever', and this they now acknowledged in regard to themselves as representing Israel. It was the confession that no merit on their side had led to the revival in which they had part. It was all on the ground of God's mercy. Every revival, granted by God, in the sad history of Christendom, has been based upon the mercy of God, without merit on our side. Let us never forget this.

There was another side to this great occasion, for there were present 'ancient men', who had seen the first house in all its magnificence, and the sound of their weeping matched the shouting of those who rejoiced, so that the two sounds were indistinguishable. The number of men, so ancient that they saw the first temple still standing, must have been small compared with the total number present, so their weeping must have been unrestrained and loud. Do we feel inclined to regard them as unthankful and melancholy, marring the brightness of a great occasion?

No, we do not. We regard them as expressing another side of things, which should ever be present, when we are able to rejoice in some time of revival, granted in the mercy of God. However blessed the revival granted, our rejoicing is tempered by the remembrance of the grace and power that characterized the beginning of things under apostolic energy, as shown in the early chapters of the Acts of the Apostles. We become conscious how small and imperfect is anything we may experience compared with that; and this, though it may not bring tears to our eyes, will have a very sobering effect upon us for our good.

CHAPTER FOUR

In the opening verses of chapter 4, another striking feature comes into view. As is always the case when a work of God takes place, there were adversaries, and their first move had in it a strong element of flattery, and was therefore a very seductive one. They came with the profession of seeking and serving the true God, and so they offered to assist in the building of the house, as being partners in the work. This brought to light a fifth feature marking this revival—a feature of great importance: Zerubbabel and Jeshua and other chief men refused the alliance they proposed, and maintained *a position of separation from the surrounding world.* Had they acquiesced, the work would have been ruined from the outset.

If we read the last chapter of the book of Nehemiah, we discover there was failure on this very point, to the marring of the work, and similarly revivals in the history of Christendom have too often been spoiled in the same way. Take the Reformation for instance: it fell very short of what it might have been as the result of many of its leaders getting into alliance with secular and worldly persons and powers, so that even religious wars were fought. That having come to pass, the power and spirituality of the revival rapidly evaporated.

Under Zerubbabel and Jeshua, however, the line of demarcation between the returned remnant of Israel and the mixed multitude that dwelt around them, was faithfully maintained, and the result of this is at once manifested. Points of dispute, which might easily lead to strife and warfare, are frequently solved, at least for a time, by a spirit of compromise. Each side yields a few points and peace is patched up; but it was not so here.

Instead of the watchword being *compromise* it was *separation*, and the result was strenuous opposition; not only weakening their hands in various ways, but also hiring counsellors against them at headquarters in a most persistent way. Here is a sixth feature that we must note. If true saints maintain separation from the world, they will have to face *opposition from the world*. This is as true today as at any other time in history. If we compromise we may avoid it in large measure and lose our power. If we maintain separation, we must face it in some way, for as the Scripture itself says, 'all that will live godly in Christ Jesus shall suffer persecution' (2 Timothy 3:12). It may not take the form of outward violence, as it did in the case of the Apostle Paul, but be exerted in more indirect and subtle ways. The absence of it would not commend us but the reverse. It would mean that the great adversary knows that as regards his designs we are innocuous, and so he wastes no energy over us.

Here it was far otherwise, and the adversary pitted his strength against those who without compromise were bent on rebuilding the house of God, as had been prophesied. The opposition was most persistent, for no less than four kings are mentioned in verses 5-7. It began at once in the days of Cyrus, and continued until the time of Darius, as stated in verse 5, who is identified as the one surnamed Hystaspes in secular history. In between these kings came Ahasuerus, not the one mentioned in the book of Esther, but the one known as Cambyses. During his reign the opponents were very active, writing up an accusation against the Jews in Jerusalem, but apparently without any definite effect.

Then came the Artaxerxes of verse 7, who is identified with the usurper, known as Smerdis in profane history, who only held dominion for a very short time. Being a usurper, he was of course disposed to upset and annul decrees of his predecessors, in order to establish, if possible, his own position. The opponents saw that this man furnished them with an excellent chance of succeeding in their petition, so once more they sent up a letter.

The opposition had not diminished by the lapse of time or by the earlier lack of success. It had rather increased, as is clear if we read verses 7-9. The letter went up in the names of certain men who were eminent amongst the inhabitants of the land, backed by no less than nine of the tribes or citizens or peoples, who then had their dwelling in the surrounding country of Palestine. It was evidently a very imposing document.

A copy of this letter is given to us in verses 11-16, that we may see how skilfully the adversary can mix lies with facts, and thus garble and misrepresent the case in question.

The first thing that strikes us is that there is no mention of the thing the Jews had come to do under the decree of Cyrus—the rebuilding of the house of God. They have much to say about the building of the city and its walls. It is possible of course that some little work of this sort had been done, which furnished them with a pretext, but we know that nothing serious of this sort was accomplished until Nehemiah's day. Their assertion of this to the king was *simply a lie.*

Then, assuming that the city was being rebuilt, they denounced it as a bad and rebellious place. It was true that the last few kings, and especially Zedekiah, had been bad men and unreliable, breaking their word in a rebellious spirit, and this gave some support to their accusation. The city, however, had originally been chosen of God and for a brief time held dominion from Him. They gained their opportunity to besmirch the whole history of Jerusalem by the bad behaviour of the last kings that reigned there: a striking example of how the whole of God's work may be dishonoured by unfaithful servants, and give the opportunity the adversary desires.

A third thing that strikes us is the way they presented the matter; as if their whole concern was for the king's advantage and reputation, and they had themselves but little interest in it. This Artaxerxes being, we understand, a usurper, he would specially fear anything that might challenge his authority. The great spiritual adversary, who lay behind these human adversaries, is not lacking in skill!

The closing verses of our chapter show that their letter had the desired effect. In those early days careful records were kept, and search being made, the unfaithful doings of Zedekiah and others were revealed, as well as records of the great dominion once exerted by such as David and Solomon. Armed with the official edict that was issued, the adversaries, 'by force and power', made the work on the house of God to cease. It seemed as if what God had purposed in this matter was effectually frustrated.

Thus it has been again and again in the sad history of the world. It appeared at the outset that God's purpose in creating Adam was defeated by the introduction of sin. It appeared as if God's call of Abram to go forth to the land of promise was defeated by his descendants going down into Egypt. It now appeared as if the establishment of God's house on earth through David and Solomon had been defeated. And so it has been in the history of Christendom, when God has intervened in reviving mercy. Always the adversary has been at work and has found human instruments available to his hand. This has been the case in our own day. We have only to consider the history of the past one hundred years—and more particularly perhaps the history of the English-speaking world—to see it all too plainly.

But does the adversary finally prevail? In the history before us the answer is found in chapters 5 and 6. When God intervenes everything is reversed. And ultimately

God always does intervene. Let us take comfort and encouragement from that.

Chapter Five

In considering the first four chapters we noted six things that marked the revival granted to the Jews, as recorded by Ezra. Let us briefly recapitulate them. There was:—

(1) A return to God's original centre.

(2) No claim to powers they had forfeited by previous failure.

(3) A spirit of devotedness and self-sacrifice.

(4) Obedience to the word of God.

(5) A position of separation from the surrounding world, and consequently,

(6) Opposition from the world.

We now begin to read chapter 5, and at once there meets us a seventh feature, which completes the picture immediately before us. The work on the house of God having ceased, because of the contrary edict from the Persian usurper, *God's Word was found in power amongst them*, through the two prophets, Haggai and Zechariah. The result of this prophetic ministry was that once more the Jews began to build the house, in spite of the contrary edict.

We have the words of these two prophets preserved for us in the books that bear their names, and if we now glance for a moment at these two prophecies, we may readily perceive their general drift or scope.

Haggai's message was a very plain word of rebuke, of instruction, of encouragement. They had stopped building the house and were engaged in building nice houses for themselves all too willingly. He told them to recommence work on the house of God, and encouraged them by predictions of future glory, though warning them that they must not imagine that anything they did was perfect. The searching eye of God could perceive uncleanness in all the works of their hands.

Zechariah's message also encouraged but had in it more of visions and symbolic instruction. He foretold the advent of the Messiah, though He would be sold for thirty pieces of silver and rejected, and the sword of Jehovah would awake against Him, so that His hand might turn in blessing upon the 'little ones', who would be marked by deep repentance. Nevertheless the Messiah would return in glory as being Jehovah Himself, and Jerusalem would ultimately become Holiness unto Jehovah.

Immediately the building of the house recommenced the adversaries were up in arms. Behind these human adversaries lay the great adversary, who does not mind God's people 'feathering their own nests', but opposes all that is for God. We may wonder perhaps that the prophets incited the people to disobey the edict against the building of the house, but God knew that the usurper being dispossessed and a king of the ancient dynasty being on the throne, the way would be clear. The Darius of verse 6, who was mentioned in verse 5 of the previous chapter, was now on the throne; and just as Artaxerxes, or Smerdis, being a usurper, was inclined to reverse the edicts of his predecessors, the new king, of the ancient line, was inclined to confirm them, and reverse the decrees of the usurper.

Hence, when fresh complaint was sent up to Darius against the Jews, now again working on the temple, he caused search to be made in the records to discover the truth of the matter. This we see in the opening verse of chapter 6, but we shall do well to take note of the ground taken by the leaders of the Jews, when confronted again by their adversaries, as recorded in the latter part of chapter 5.

Their opponents put on record that when challenged their answer was twofold; both religious and political; and they put the religious reason in the first place, saying, 'We are the servants of the God of heaven and earth', and are building under His command. In the second place they quoted the original authorization they had received from Cyrus.

Their position was indeed a strong one. Centuries later Peter and the other apostles were challenged by the Jewish council in the effort to stop them preaching the risen Christ, and thus working in the spiritual building, that started on the day when the Spirit was poured forth, as narrated in Acts 2. Their answer was, 'We ought to obey God rather than men' (Acts 5:29); and so they continued to preach the Gospel in spite of the prohibition issued by the religious authorities. Here, however, the verdict of Darius was entirely favourable. He cancelled the adverse command and confirmed the original edict of Cyrus. Thus God caused the wrath of men to praise Him, and fulfil His word.

CHAPTER SIX

The original decree of Cyrus having been discovered, it was found to be more full in its details and more favourable to the Jews than their adversaries had imagined. It demanded not only that they be left unhindered, but rather actively helped in their work, and be supplied with things needed; and that all who set themselves to hinder or destroy should themselves be destroyed and their houses made a dunghill.

So it came to pass that the house was built in the course of a good many years, for it was not finished until the sixth year of Darius, as verse 15 tells us. When completed there was a season of much joy, sacrifices were offered and the Passover was observed, as recorded in the closing verses of chapter 6. Two things marked the people, which we shall do well to note. First, the Passover was eaten not only by the children of Israel, who had come out of captivity, but also by 'all such as had separated themselves unto them from the filthiness of the heathen of the land, to seek the Lord God of Israel'. We learn from Jeremiah 52:16, that when the great captivity took place, 'certain of the poor of the land' were left unremoved, that they might be husbandmen and carry on cultivation. Some of these, or their descendants, cleansed themselves from evils in which they had become involved, and joined in this time of revival and blessing, and so could take part in the feast of unleavened bread.

A second thing, which points in the same direction, we see in an earlier verse. They rightly discerned that, in view of the sad and sinful history of the nation a sin offering was necessary, if they were solemnly to place themselves thus before the God of their fathers; but this they offered in 'twelve he goats, according to the number of the tribes of Israel', though the mass of those who had come out of captivity were of the tribes of Judah and Benjamin.

By this time five or six centuries had elapsed since the rending of the nation and the secession of the ten tribes under Jeroboam, but the returned remnant recognized that God had called the whole nation out of Egypt, that the division that had ensued was their failure and not God's purpose, and that God never swerves from His original thought and call. Hence they still had all twelve tribes on their hearts. Though they were but a remnant, they held to God's thought and purpose for the whole nation.

This has a very distinct voice to us today. The divisions of Christendom are multiplied, but if saints are found, bearing a remnant character, in keeping with what we are seeing in the book of Ezra, they must ever keep in view the whole Church of God, and not become wrapped up in themselves, as though others did not count before God. Every available Israelite, who was clean, by having separated himself from the filthiness of the surrounding heathen, was to benefit by the sacrifices offered, and participate in the feasts of the Passover and of Unleavened Bread.

Chapter Seven

It was after these things, as the first verse of chapter 7 tells us, that Ezra the priest with Levitical companions left Babylon and went up to Jerusalem. It was in the seventh year of that Artaxerxes, under whom thirteen years later Nehemiah went up. Ezra's genealogy was clearly known, and it is given in the first 5 verses, showing him to be truly descended from Aaron, the first high priest. This fact qualified him for the place he was about to take. He had the further qualification of being, 'a ready scribe in the law of Moses', which indicates that he was fully acquainted with the original word of God, which still had authority over the lives of the people.

But he had a third qualification of even greater importance, and this is stated in verse 10. He was a man who *prepared his heart*, which indicates that he was a man of spiritual exercise, something like Timothy of New Testament days, who was to meditate upon the things of God and give himself wholly to them. As a scribe he must have had a good knowledge of the words he had often written, and this must have prepared his *head*. The preparing of his *heart* went much deeper than this, for it led him to *seek* the law of the Lord'. He really wanted to be instructed of God.

The next statement of verse 10 still further deepens his qualifications. He was a seeker after the law in order that he might *do it*. This was the crowning feature that marked him. Let us pause and consider this.

Ezra lived under the law of Moses, in regard to which our Lord said, 'This do, and thou shalt live' (Luke 10:28), and he knew well that to do it was the great thing. We are not under the law but under grace, yet we have the apostolic injunction, 'Be ye *doers* of the word, and not hearers only, deceiving your own selves' (James 1:22). In this Paul does indeed agree with James, for in all his epistles he first expounds doctrine and then enforces the practical living and behaviour that the doctrine demands. Under the law men were to *do* in order to live. Under the Gospel we are brought into life in order that we may *do* the will of God. It is easy to forget this, and treat Christianity as though it were simply an exalted philosophy to entertain our minds.

Having prepared his heart to seek the law, so that he might do it, and thus exemplify its demands to some degree, he was now in the right state to 'teach in Israel statutes and judgments.' We all can see the point of this, and we trust we may realize its implications in regard to ourselves. We only effectually teach if our own lives are in accordance with what we say. How well the Apostle Paul illustrated this, for twice he alluded to it: when speaking to the elders of Ephesus: I 'have shewed you, and have taught you', and again, 'I have shewed you all things' (Acts 20:20, 35). He illustrated in his life what he taught with his mouth. This is the effective way of teaching, whether it be in Ezra's day, or Paul's, or our own.

Following this statement of the piety and zeal that marked Ezra, we have given us a full account of the letter given by Artaxerxes to Ezra, amounting to a decree, under the authority of which he journeyed to Jerusalem and acted when he got there. It occupies verses 11-26. As one reads through these verses, one cannot but be struck with the wonderful work of God in the mind of a heathen king, which led him to grant such powers, order such assistance to be given and express such a recognition of the claims and greatness of 'the God of heaven'. We also see the overruling wisdom of God controlling the mind of the king so that His servant was given liberty, and even commanded, to do what God proposed.

Ezra, we see, was given remarkable authority, it being assumed that he would act, as the king said, 'after the wisdom of thy God'; and he and his helpers were exempted from every form of tax or exaction, and also given power to punish all evildoers, whether they transgressed the law of God or 'the law of the king'. Ezra was to teach the laws of God to those who were ignorant of them. So Ezra was commissioned to go up to the land armed with remarkable powers in the providence of God.

The two verses that close this chapter record Ezra's thanksgiving as he recognized how God had put His good hand upon him and moved the king's heart to grant all this. All was 'to beautify the house of the Lord'. The silver and gold and other gifts out of the treasuries would doubtless be used to increase the natural beauty of the house that was being constructed, but we venture to think that the teaching of the law, which Ezra purposed to do, would produce in the people, if they received it, a piety, which is a greater adornment to any house than can be conferred by any amount of silver and gold. The piety that marked Ezra himself can be plainly seen in these two verses.

CHAPTER EIGHT

The first fourteen verses are occupied with the names of those who accompanied Ezra according to their genealogies, and with the number of the males in each family. God has seen to it that the names of those who bestirred themselves to answer to His call to return to the land, should be placed on record in a very permanent way, while the names of those who did not bestir themselves are almost entirely lost.

With verse fifteen we resume the history of the migration; how again, as is confessed, 'by the good hand of our God upon us', there was brought to them the 'man of understanding' that they needed, so that all together they were gathered at the river of Ahava, ready to set forth. Ezra recognized, however, that the fact that they had very definitely received help of God in the past did not exempt them from the need of dependence on Him for the present, hence His face must again be sought before they started; so according to the customs of the law a fast was proclaimed that they might afflict their souls before God, and seek of Him the right way for their journey.

Journeying in those days was not particularly safe or easy, so worldly prudence would have dictated the request of an armed escort. This Ezra did not do, and in verse 22 we have his touching confession in the matter. He had spoken in very definite fashion to the king as to the care of his God on behalf of His people and His wrath against those who forsake Him, so he was ashamed to depart in practice from what he had professed. This frank confession on Ezra's part sets before us a very good example. He was on God's business, and so did not need to rely on worldly support.

Let us consider how easy it is for us in our day to profess much confidence in God as to how we carry on His work, and yet to fail when the test comes, and we are faced with some very practical questions. We may well be ashamed when some adversary can reproach us by calling upon us to *practise* what we *preach*. If we take the Apostle Paul as an example, as well as Ezra, it is quite plain that in carrying on the work of God we do not need the support nor the patronage of the world.

Being assured that God had heard their entreaty, Ezra gave into the hands of trusted helpers the gold and silver treasures they had with them, and they started on their journey from Ahava, and safely arrived at Jerusalem with everything intact. Those to whom the treasure had been entrusted had proved faithful, and they returned thanks to God by their burnt offerings. Thus far all was well.

But the next chapter is going to record for us the shock that awaited Ezra when Jerusalem was entered.

CHAPTER NINE

The history of all the revivals, that God grants in His mercy, seems to be the same: a bright beginning, followed by declension more or less rapid. There is this constant tendency to forsake the fountain of living waters, and hew ourselves out broken cisterns that can hold no water (see Jeremiah 2:13). Thus it has been from ancient times to our own day. Many of us may have inherited good things from more recent revivals, granted in the mercy of God; but how are we holding and profiting by these things? Or, are we neglecting them and letting them slip away?

Ezra had been so prospered of God in the enterprise he had undertaken that he may well have arrived in Jerusalem with high hopes. If so, the information he at once received must have come to him with very painful force. Among the people then in the land, there were certain princes who realized the sad declension that had taken place. That which had started so brightly under Zerubbabel and Jeshua had been gravely marred. Not only the common people, but also priests, Levites, and even princes and rulers, had been involved in the trespass. They had failed to maintain the necessary separation from the varied heathen nations that surrounded them. Intermarrying with them, they had learned their customs and had practised their abominable sacrifices and ways.

If we read the first six verses of Deuteronomy 7, we find that seven nations, who were greater and mightier than Israel, were in the land that God had given to them; they were to destroy them and contract no marriages with them, so that they might not be perverted to their ways. Even under the faithful Joshua this was only partially done, and now many centuries later we see the effects of their failure. In the first verse of our chapter the nations mentioned are almost the same as those we find in Deuteronomy 7, and to them the Egyptians are added, making eight in all.

The people had been warned through Moses of the disastrous effects that would flow from alliance with these peoples, and those effects had come to pass in the history of both the ten tribes and the two, and had led to the scattering and the captivity. Now once again the same snare had entangled the returned remnant, in spite of a bright start, and hearing of it, Ezra was overwhelmed.

And we have painfully to reflect that the same snare, though it is mainly exercised in a rather different way, underlies much of the almost apostate conditions that prevail in Christendom today. The evil set in when there was the merging of the Church and the world under the Roman Emperor Constantine, which in the course of a few centuries led to the rise of the Papacy as a great world-power. And later again, after the Reformation, state churches came into existence, in which those truly converted and the unconverted are mixed together, and so on. The damaging effect of this is all too evident on every hand.

Have our eyes been opened to see the terrible failure that has marked the church in this thing? And if we have seen it, have our reactions been at all similar to that displayed by Ezra? We fear it has not been so. We shall do well to take very careful notice of the effect which the sad discovery had upon him.

Here was a man singularly free from the evil that was uncovered before him, yet he smote himself, instead of starting to smite the guilty parties. According to the customs of those days, he rent his clothes, but not content with this he smote himself, by plucking out hair from his head and beard—a painful process. Having done so, he sat down 'astonied', or 'overwhelmed'. He began with himself in humiliation before God.

Starting thus, the effect was immediate. Amongst the returned remnant there were those who were conscious of the widespread transgression of the law in this matter, but who had not the energy, and perhaps not the position among the people, to do anything about it. These were at once stirred up by Ezra's drastic action, and identified themselves with him, as verse 4 records. They were those who 'trembled at the words of the God of Israel', and these, being like Ezra, are just the people to whom God will look in His mercy, as stated in Isaiah 66:2.

At the time of the evening sacrifice, when there was a small typical representation of the sacrifice of Christ, Ezra arose with his rent garments and fell on his knees to approach God in the remarkable prayer, which is recorded in verses 6-15; a prayer in which no actual request was made; consisting as it did from first to last in humble and heart-broken confession of sins, in which he personally had not shared.

One remarkable feature, characterizing the whole confession, is that he identified himself with the people, and confessed the evils as though they were his own. From beginning to end he uses 'we' and 'us', where we might have expected 'they' and 'them' to appear. Moreover he acknowledged that the evils that had confronted him were a reviving of the sins that had defiled his people from the outset, or as he put it, 'since the days of our fathers', but aggravated by the fact that they were being repeated after God had shown such mercy in relieving them of the governmental consequences of their former sins.

This prayer of Ezra contains admonition for ourselves of a solemnizing kind, so we do well to consider it. In the history of Christendom great mercy has been shown, and from the time of the Reformation revivings have taken place, but only to be marked by this same tendency to revert to former evils. It would indeed be well if every true saint today was on his or her knees before God with words like Ezra's, springing from convictions and a heart like his. And all too often we should have to make our confession as having been involved in the sin and defilement, and not, like Ezra, as identifying ourselves with those who have done so.

CHAPTER TEN

In verse 1, we see Ezra on his knees, and as he confessed, moved by deep emotion that revealed itself in weeping. Some of us are so constituted that we dislike anything emotional, but we must recognize that truly deep conviction, whether as to things good or things evil, is bound to produce emotion—an example of emotion in both directions is found in 2 Timothy 1:4. Paul was not a mere theologian, propounding Christian doctrine in a philosophical way, but an ardent servant of Christ, moved in his spirit by what he preached and by the needs of both saints and sinners. Timothy too he commended as one who would 'care with genuine feeling how ye get on' (Philippians 2:20, New Trans.). Let us cultivate today a similar tenderness of feeling.

We should then be more likely to see our attitude and words having real effect upon others, as is recorded in the case of Ezra. The fact was quickly revealed that in Israel there were a large number who were aware of the sin and departure but had not the faith and spiritual energy to act as he did. Awakened to the sin and need by him, they also assembled and wept as he did. And further than this, a leader amongst them declared that the only hope lay in putting away the evils in which they had been involved and obeying the instructions they had been given from the outset. He reminded them in effect of what the Lord had said through Jeremiah, recorded in verse 16 of his sixth chapter. The principle there stated stands good today. At the beginning of each dispensation God makes known the 'paths' that suit what He has introduced and established. These remain unchanged throughout the dispensation, and to revert to them after a season of departure is always right. Let us see that we do so today.

A special responsibility rested upon Ezra in this matter, since as we saw in the early part of chapter 7, he had prepared his heart to *seek*, and *do*, and *teach* the law of the Lord. This was recognized by Shechaniah, so that he said to him, 'Arise; for this matter belongeth unto thee'; and he assured him he would have the support of those who feared God in the action that he had to take.

Thus God wrought in that day, and it does seem to be His normal way of working. Not every Christian is qualified and called to initiate some work of God, not even in the early days. Hence that word, 'Remember your leaders who have spoken to you the word of God' (Hebrews 13:7). The word to be emphasized here is 'Leaders', for they not only expounded the way, and enforced it by word of mouth, but *walked in it* themselves.

In the case before us Ezra's action and words had a remarkable and immediate effect, for God was with him. On a large scale the people were moved and trembled as they realized how they had disobeyed the law, and a great rain from heaven heightened their distress. The resolution was made to confess their trespass and to put away their connections with the heathen women, in which they had been entangled.

These two things appear in verse 11. It is sadly possible to make confession of wrong-doing, and yet continue in it in more subtle and unseen ways. It is also possible to realize that wrong-doing of a certain sort is not profitable and to forsake it, but without any confession of wrong in the matter. But when the conviction of sin is genuine, there is first confession of the sin, and then a forsaking of it, as is plainly intimated in Proverbs 28:13.

The rest of this chapter, and indeed of the book, is taken up with two things. First, we are told of the careful and orderly way in which was effected the difficult and distressing work of putting away the strange wives, and thus delivering themselves from this worldly and sinful entanglement. Had it been done in an impulsive and reckless way, it might have brought further dishonour on the name of the Lord. This too may have a voice for us. As we grow in grace and our understanding of the will of God is enlarged, we may become aware that something, that we thought little of, is really a spiritual entanglement and hindrance. Let us get out of it in a way that is worthy of the Lord whom we serve and obey. If, for instance, it means loss being incurred somewhere, let us accept the loss ourselves, instead of imposing it upon others.

The second thing, with which the book closes, is a lengthy list of those who had been involved in the trespass. It may surprise us to see that the first names mentioned in verse 18, were sons of Jeshua the son of Jozadak, the man whose name follows that of Zerubbabel in chapter 2:2; the priest who is mentioned in the prophecy of Haggai, and again in Zechariah 3. Some, if not all his sons, had taken part in this sin. But really, this should not surprise us, for similar tragedies have been all too frequent. We have only to cite the cases of Aaron and his two sons, of Samuel and his sons, of Eli and his sons, of David and his sons, of Hezekiah and his son Manasseh. And so we might continue even to recent times. It is a sad and humbling fact that many true and devoted servants of our Lord have had sons who have not followed in their father's footsteps. The recognition of this fact should lead us to be much in prayer for the families of those who serve the Lord Jesus.

Lastly, notice that the names given are of those who *put away* the strange wives, and offered a *trespass offering*. It was surely to their discredit that they had taken these wives, but the putting away of them was to their credit, and so their names appear in the record. They were, as we might now put it, backsliders restored, as the result of the faithful ministry and action of Ezra. He had indeed been, 'a ready scribe in the law of Moses'.

Nehemiah

CHAPTER ONE

In the first chapter we find ourselves carried to the 20th year of Artaxerxes, whereas Ezra went to Jerusalem in the 7th year of that king. Nehemiah was not a priest, but he was at Shushan the palace in an official capacity. His story begins when certain Jews arrived, who had knowledge of the condition of things prevailing then at Jerusalem, and he enquired of them as to the state of the remnant that had returned there years before, and as to the conditions prevailing in the city. The answer of these men is given to us in verse 3.

Their report was a distressful one. Jerusalem as a city was still in a ruinous state, and the people there in great affliction and reproach. The effect this news had upon Nehemiah is related in the rest of the chapter. We venture to think it should also have a very definite effect upon us.

We have just seen in the book of Ezra how under God-fearing men, Zerubbabel and Jeshua, a remnant had returned and rebuilt the temple, and though defection supervened in the course of years, the coming of Ezra led to a distinct reformation; yet now, thirteen years after, they are marked by affliction and reproach. We might have expected that instead of this God would have rewarded them by visible tokens of His approval and favour.

The next book, that of Esther, relates for us things that happened to the much larger number of Jews, that did not concern themselves with God's interests in His temple, but preferred to remain in the land of their captivity, where in the course of the seventy years many of them had settled down in comparative prosperity. The name of God is not mentioned in Esther, and we might have expected that these easy-going folk would have come under His displeasure. What do we find? Read Esther 9:17-19, and see. The people who, in spite of their defects, had cared for God's interests and rebuilt His temple, marked by affliction and reproach; while those who did not concern themselves, remaining in their comforts, have 'feasting', 'gladness', and 'a good day'.

What instruction shall we gather from this extraordinary and, we venture to think, this unexpected contrast? Well, in the first place, worldly prosperity and jollification, even if the fruit of God's care and dealings behind the scenes, is not necessarily an indication of His approval, nor is affliction a sign of His disapproval, as is seen in far more striking degree in the case of Job. Secondly, we may refer to what is stated in Hebrews 12:6, 'Whom the Lord loveth He chasteneth'. If we read Psalm 73, we find the same problem exercising the mind of the writer. He saw those who definitely were wicked prospering, while the godly were chastened. It was when he went into the sanctuary of God that he found the solution.

Nehemiah of course had not the light that the New Testament sheds upon this problem, so the sad tidings concerning, 'the remnant that are left', affected him deeply, for in spirit he was *of* them, though not actually *with* them. He was moved to *tears, mourning, fasting* and *prayer*. The report he had heard was mainly concerned with the outward circumstances of the remnant, rather than with their inward spiritual state, but it moved him to these four things.

And what about present-day conditions among the true saints of God? Many are in outward affliction under the iron hand of Communism or Romanism, while in the English-speaking world the increased inflow of money into our pockets seems to have produced a decreased outflow of love and devotion from our souls. Have these four things ever marked us? Have we ever mourned to tears over the thousands of our fellow-saints persecuted and even martyred in this century? Have we ever abstained from lawful things and given ourselves to prayer on their behalf? The writer leaves each reader to answer these questions for himself. He knows quite well what he would have to reply.

The prayer of Nehemiah, though shorter than Ezra's, is very similar. He too identified himself with the sin of the people, saying, '*we* have sinned'. But in one direction he went further, pleading the word of the Lord, that had been written in Leviticus 26. Israel had been warned that disobedience to the law would bring upon themselves a scattering; but that even then if they turned to God in obedience to His word, He would gather them from distant lands and restore them to the place of His name. On this, which had been written, he based his plea. For those in Jerusalem and for himself he made the claim that they were those, 'who desire to fear Thy name'.

While making request in a more general way for the returned remnant in Jerusalem, he had a more definite request to make for himself. He was in a post of special responsibility before the king, and having access to his presence, he intended to make a request of the monarch that he might very naturally entirely refuse. He sought therefore that God would prosper him in that which he had in mind.

CHAPTER TWO

The king's cup-bearer of those days had to be a man of integrity, who would see that nothing undesirable or poisonous was inserted into the King's wine. The tidings he had just received had so affected him that his sorrow was seen in his face. Noticing it, the king was of course suspicious and enquired what moved him to sorrow; as we see in the opening verses of chapter 2. A position was thus created that had definite danger in it, and Nehemiah was 'very sore afraid'. However, he told the king of the tidings that he had received, which accounted for his sad countenance that had revealed the sadness of his heart.

The king did show him mercy as he had desired, and invited a request from him. This was a challenge, and Nehemiah's response to it is very instructive. The record is, first, 'So I prayed to the God of heaven', and then, 'I said to the king ...'. God first, and the king second. This silent prayer must have shot up to heaven in a matter of two or three seconds, quite unknown to the king or anybody else, and it was evidently as speedily answered from heaven, so that the request he made was the right one, and to meet with a favourable answer.

Would to God that we and all other true saints of God were so truly and simply living in touch with our Lord on high that in any and every emergency, needing a quick decision, we could at once with a minimum of words, remit the case to Him for His decision, and guidance for ourselves. We should more often see His hand moving on our behalf, even as for Nehemiah: as the rest of the story unfolds.

Invited by the king to make a request, Nehemiah asked, with due deference, that he might be permitted to go to Jerusalem with the king's authority to rebuild it; that authority to be expressed in letters, not only to Asaph, the keeper of the king's forest, but also to governors beyond the river. The 'river' here is doubtless the Euphrates, and so the governors were those that ruled in the direction of Palestine. What considerations moved the king's mind are hidden from us, that we may more clearly realize that, whatever they were, it was the power of God that controlled him, in response to Nehemiah's brief and sudden prayer.

The king was so favourable to Nehemiah's request that he sent captains and horsemen to speed him on his way. We may remember that though Ezra had returned earlier under the same king, carrying much treasure under his authority, he had not requested such official protection, since he had openly avowed his faith in the protection of God during his journey. Evidently Nehemiah, an official in the king's court, had not the spiritual education and understanding that Ezra possessed as a priest, devoted to the law of his God, yet both equally could speak of 'the good hand of my God upon me.' If the heart be right, God will guide and support His servant, whatever be the measure of his intelligence and faith. This fact should encourage us today. Our faith and understanding may indeed be small, but let us see that our hearts are marked by true devotion to Christ and His present interests. As the fruit of devotion, intelligence will surely increase.

But, immediately there is action, as the result of devotion and some understanding, opposition is sure to appear. It had been so when at the start of the revival Zerubbabel and his party went back; it was so again, as verse 10 reveals, though the men who led the opposition were different. Sanballat was an Horonite; that is, we understand, an inhabitant of Horonaim, a town of Moab; while Tobiah was an Ammonite. So here we have representatives of the two sons of Lot, begotten under shameful circumstances, as recorded in Genesis 19, setting themselves against what God was doing. A man had come 'to seek the welfare of the children of Israel', which at that moment God had in view, and therefore the adversary was against it, and used these two men, who as to their origins were distant relations of Israel. It has often been the case, sad to say, that those nearly related to the saints of God have been foremost in their opposition against them.

It is worthy of note that this antagonism existed before Nehemiah revealed the exact purpose for which he had come. He abode in Jerusalem three days and then he arose secretly in the night and made a tour of the city that he might see for himself the exact state of things. The rulers of the Jews, as we are told in verse 16, had no knowledge of what he did, nor of the plan before him. It was only when he had seen the state of things for himself, that he set before them what he proposed, and said, 'let us build up the wall of Jerusalem, that we be no more a reproach.'

The building of the wall was then the great object before him. The house of the Lord had already been built, but it stood in a desolated place, the walls of which were broken down and its gates consumed by fire. The day had not come then, nor has it come yet, when 'the Lord will be unto her a wall of fire round about, and will be the glory in the midst of her' (Zechariah 2:5), so a wall was needed that the city might again be seen as the place where God had set *His* name, and His house might, in this typical way, be separated from the defilements of the surrounding world. From the time that God said to Abram, 'Get thee out …' (Genesis 12:1), separation to Himself has always been God's mind for His people. Since the rejection of Christ this has come to light with increased emphasis, so that we now read, 'the friendship of the world is enmity with God' (James 4:4).

Having proposed the rebuilding of the wall, Nehemiah was able to tell the rulers, 'of the hand of my God, which was good upon me'. This plainly conveyed to them that God was behind the project, and they responded, saying, 'Let us rise up and build.' They were prepared really to put their hands to the work. Pious thoughts and understanding are not enough. They had to put their hands to the task, and work. It is even thus with us today. To understand God's mind and purpose is not enough; we must be prepared to give ourselves to the active service which is indicated. Here, we fear, is a very weak spot in many Christian lives.

As it became increasingly plain that work was really going to be undertaken, so the opposition increased, and in verse 19 we find Geshem the Arabian joining with the Moabite and the Ammonite. This is remarkable for the inhabitants of Arabia were largely the descendants of Ishmael and Esau, and to this day the bitterest foes of the Jews are the various Arab tribes. And further, in prophetic scriptures Edom, Moab and Ammon are linked together. In the coming day, according to Daniel 11:41, the king of the north will overthrow many lands, but these three will escape him; only to be subdued by Israel, regathered and unified, according to Isaiah 11:14.

In our chapter, however, the opposition for the moment only took the form of mockery— 'they laughed us to scorn, and despised us'. This type of opposition all too often has considerable effect, even upon the people of God; but only if they are living and acting as before men. Nehemiah and his friends were acting as before God in what they proposed to do, as we see in the last verse of our chapter. Their reply was, 'The God of heaven, He will prosper us'. They anticipated in their measure the triumphant word of Romans 8:31. 'If God be for us, who can be against us?' In the light of that they were about to act; and they reminded the adversaries how complete was the breach that lay between them and themselves.

We may take the three things that Nehemiah mentioned as having an application at the present time. It is as true today as when the Psalmist wrote, that 'men of the world', who so often oppose Christ and His saints, 'have their portion in this life' (Psalm 17:14), and no portion at all in the things of God. Hence in these things they have no 'right', and their thoughts and opinions are valueless. Nor, when the things of God are finally established in glory, will they have any 'memorial' therein. They will be outside it all for ever. Let us never be diverted from the work of God, nor even ashamed, by the ridicule of men, who oppose Christ and His service.

CHAPTER THREE

Chapter 3 is occupied with details concerning the actual building of the wall, but in it are placed on record some things that are of interest to us today. We note first of all, that God has seen fit to occupy a whole chapter in recording the names of the leaders of families or townships, who engaged in it. We might wonder that so much valuable space should be taken up with the names of men, who would otherwise be forgotten. We deduce from it however the fact that the humblest service for the will of God is not forgotten but put on record, especially when carried on in the face of ridicule and opposition.

The whole chapter appears to us as like a miniature forecast of the judgment-seat of Christ. This is specially so, when we read verses 5, 12, 20, 23 and 27. The Tekoites were very diligent, for they repaired 'another piece', as well as the first they undertook; yet it is recorded that 'their nobles put not their necks to the work of their Lord'. All too often worldly elevation proves a hindrance when the work of the Lord is in question. Their 'nobles', no doubt liked to talk and direct, but did not like to soil their hands, nor bend their necks, *to do the work*.

On the other hand, there was Shallum, who was ruler of the half part of Jerusalem, putting his hand to the work, and not only he but *his daughters* also. These 'daughters' remind us of the two women who 'laboured' with Paul 'in the Gospel', according to Philippians 4:2-3. What counts with God is devotion and earnestness. So the work of these daughters has a place in the record, and similar devotion and work in the present interests of the Lord, will find mention and reward at the judgment-seat of Christ.

This thought is reinforced by the case of Baruch the son of Zabbai, for it is recorded that he '*earnestly* repaired the other piece'. He was evidently marked by unusual zeal, and it is noted and placed on the record: just as it is recorded of some of the workers, including even some of the priests, that they repaired 'against their house', which of course meant that they concerned themselves with the section that was of most interest and convenience *to themselves*. To do this was not so praise-worthy as to work on some piece of no particular interest to the worker; or perhaps even repulsive, as for instance, the repairing of the 'dung gate', undertaken by a man who was a ruler of part of a township, as is recorded in verse 14.

So the reading of this chapter should remind us that today we are called to serve the Lord's interests, either by building or maintaining the wall of separation, that surrounds God's present 'house', which is the church of God, protecting it from the defilements of 'this present evil world'. It should remind us also of the truth stated by the godly woman, Hannah, in her prayer, placed on record in 1 Samuel 2, that, 'The Lord is a God of knowledge, and by Him actions are weighed'. When our actions, as we seek to serve the Lord, are weighed, how will they appear—weighty, or of little worth?

Chapter Four

When the work of building was really started, the anger and opposition of the adversaries was much increased, as chapter 4 records. All this was expressed in a threefold way. First there was *mockery*. The Jews were indeed feeble and their work of reviving 'the stones out of the heaps of the rubbish which are burned', did seem a fantastic enterprise, and the adversaries made the most of it by way of ridicule. But further there was *misrepresentation*, regarding the objects before them in their work; and then the opposition took an active form in preparation to intervene by *force*, and fight against them.

We may trace similar opposition by the great adversary in this our Gospel age. We see it in the service of the Apostle Paul. Delivering his message in cultured Athens, he was derided as a 'babbler' (Acts 17:18). Again before Festus he was considered 'mad' (Acts 26:24). Here was ridicule. In Thessalonica there was misrepresentation, for he was imagined to be turning 'the world upside down', and doing things, 'contrary to the decrees of Caesar' (Acts 17:6-7). Neither assertion was true. The Gospel leaves the world-system untouched, but calls individuals out of the world, turning them right side up, according to God. Then the violent opposition of the adversary was seen in the sufferings he had to endure, a list of which he was inspired to place on record in 2 Corinthians 11:24-27. If we in our day were more energetic and more faithful in our service for the Lord Jesus, we should doubtless know more of all three things.

In the latter part of the chapter we learn the measures that were taken in the presence of all this. First of all there was *prayer* made to God, as verse 9 records. A very right move! Nehemiah began with prayer, as we saw at the start of the story, and in a prayerful spirit they continued. Have we not often made the mistake in some emergency of taking certain steps that to us seemed reasonable and prudent, and then praying afterwards that God would bless what we have done. In His mercy He may so bless, but we should have done better if we had prayed first.

Then they faced the difficulties of the work. There was much rubbish that hindered and caused the strength of workers to fail, and the adversaries prepared to attack them. We venture to draw an analogy here. Their work was one of revival—reviving the wall that separated the temple of God from the outside world. In the mercy of God various revivals have been granted in the history of the professing church, and every time there has been more or less 'rubbish', that needed to be removed. What a terrible accumulation of worldly and moral rubbish, for instance, had been heaped up by Papal Rome, during the thousand years or more that preceded the revival that we speak of as the Reformation. And not all by any means, was actually removed then; the strength of the workers failed before it was accomplished. We Christians have always to watch against the accumulation of this kind of rubbish.

Then the opponents threatened actual attack of a violent sort, and against this the Jews armed themselves. In their case of course such arms as the world then used—spears, swords, etc.—were taken both by the would-be attackers and the defenders. In our age the more dangerous form of attack is of a spiritual sort. Servants of God, even in our day, have been slain, but 'the blood of the martyrs is the seed of the church', which has been proved again and again. The sword to be used, in meeting the spiritual attack, is 'the word of God', as plainly declared in Ephesians 6:17, where the spiritual conflict is stressed.

In English-speaking lands, where religious liberty is freely granted, the conflict side of Christian life is apt to be overlooked, and the idea entertained that our pilgrimage to a joyous heaven is to be happy and serene. But such is not the prospect held out in Scripture. We are not only pilgrims but also disciples, who are called to take up our cross in following our rejected Lord, and as identified with Him, conflict is inevitable. As 'a good soldier of Jesus Christ' we are to 'endure hardness' (2 Timothy 2:3), consequently the protective armour of Ephesians 6 is needed, as well as the 'sword of the Spirit', for offensive action.

The courage that marked Nehemiah and his helpers is seen very clearly in verse 14; a courage which sprang from the call to 'remember the Lord, which is great and terrible', who was on their side. The result was that the building of the wall did not cease, though perhaps it proceeded more slowly, since defence was necessary. The workers, whether bearers of burdens or builders, had to carry weapons, and so each had only one hand for the work, the other holding a sword. Thus it is stated in verse 17.

Thus too it has been during the church's history, even to our own times. True servants of God have always had to spend a substantial portion of their time and energy in defence of the truth. From the beginning the apostles had not only to evangelize and teach the truth; they had to spend much time in defending it from the attacks of the adversary, as the epistles bear witness. There was, if we remember aright, not so long ago a magazine entitled 'Sword and Trowel', produced by the well-known C. H. Spurgeon, who with all his preaching gift had to contend earnestly for the faith in his closing days. The title of the magazine was doubtless taken from the chapter we are considering. The truth is worth contending for. If we lose it we lose practically everything. So let us each see to it that in a spiritual sense we have a sword in one hand, while in the other we have a trowel, wherewith to do the work of the Lord.

At the end of our chapter we notice another thing. Beside the sword and the trowel there was the trumpet, which was to be blown when an alarm was necessary. The work was great and large, so that the workers were widely separated, one from the other, yet they were one in the work, and not a number of disconnected individuals. Hence what endangered one endangered all, and their unity in the work was to be preserved. Here again we see an important lesson, that we very much need to bear in mind, in order to act on it.

This oneness of action in the service of God is specially important for us, and that for two reasons. First, because the oneness of saints today, brought into the church of God, is much more fully stressed than it was with the twelve tribes of Israel. This is seen in the Ephesian epistle—read Ephesians 2:14-18, where the word 'one' occurs four times; and Ephesians 4:3-6, where it occurs seven times. Second, because the present service of God is so varied, as we see in 1 Corinthians 12. There is great diversity in the unity, so that the human body is used to illustrate it, and no one member can dispense with the service of another without damage and loss. The trumpet on the walls of Jerusalem reminds us that if the enemy set himself to attack one of the small groups of workers, he was really attacking all.

In the closing verse of our chapter we get a glimpse of the great zeal and devotion that characterized Nehemiah and his helpers. All of them were to lodge inside Jerusalem, thus obtaining such protection as the partly built walls could offer, and none of them put off their clothes, so as to sleep with comfort by night, though they removed them for personal cleanliness. They were therefore always ready to labour in the work and to meet the foe. A very impressive picture!

Vigilance and *purity* are two things very necessary for us. We see them impressed on Timothy by Paul. If we read 2 Timothy 2:21, we find he was to be vigilant as to error of a fundamental sort, and 'purge' himself out from it. Then, reading the next verse, we find he was to 'flee also youthful lusts', so that his personal cleanliness might be maintained, in a spiritual way.

And the instructions given to Timothy in the first century are in this century equally important for us.

CHAPTER FIVE

We have noticed certain good features that marked the people, as recorded in chapter 4, but as we commence to read chapter 5, we discover that beneath the surface sad mischief had been at work. Under Nehemiah's leadership there had been a courageous attitude towards opposition from *without*, while all the time there was selfish oppression proceeding *within*. The richer Jews had taken advantage of the plight into which many poorer ones had drifted, owing to the shortage of the necessaries of life, borrowing money or raising mortgages, in order to obtain food for themselves and their families. We might summarize the situation by saying that while externally they presented a picture of commendable zeal, in doing what was God's service at that moment, internally they were guilty of much self-seeking and corruption.

The Apostle Paul reminded Timothy that the 'Holy Scriptures', which he had known 'from a child', —the Old Testament, therefore—were able to make him 'wise unto salvation' (2 Timothy 3:15); not only from future doom, but also from the dangers that infest our pilgrim path. Here, we think, is an illustration of this, for again and again even in our day, the work of God in revival amongst His saints has been damaged in similar fashion. Whilst outwardly the work of God has been carried on with diligence and success, even in building a wall of spiritual separation from the outside world; there has grown up the spirit of self-seeking within, and consequently of damage and impoverishment to many humbler saints. Is not this the reason why gracious revivals, that have visited the English-speaking regions during the past four centuries, have lost their power and gradually faded away?

So, in the light of what is here recorded, let us all accept the warning, and try our ways before our Lord. In the case before us the situation was met for a time by the faithful energy of Nehemiah. He was angry, with the kind of anger that is to be permitted, as Ephesians 4:26 indicates, and he called upon them to act 'in the fear of God', even if they did not fear the retribution of men. Faced by Nehemiah's searching words, they had nothing to say. They admitted the charge, and under an oath they undertook to restore what they had taken away, and this they did according to the 13th verse.

What added force to Nehemiah's indignant charge was that he himself had been so careful in this matter, as we see in the verses that follow. Former governors had exacted their food and support from the people. He on the contrary had taken nothing from them, and had supported 150 Jews and rulers, besides occasional visitors. Just how he did this we are not told, but presumably he drew his supplies from the Persian monarch. When rebuke is called for, the power of it is greatly increased when the one administering it is wholly free of the error he has to rebuke. The same principle stands when the happy work of restoration has to be undertaken, as we see in Galatians 6:1— 'considering thyself, lest thou also be tempted'. Either way, the call to consider ourselves and our own ways is very insistent, when dealing with others. This integrity also gave Nehemiah confidence in calling upon God for good, as the last verse of the chapter shows.

CHAPTER SIX

Chapter 6 discloses to us that, as the building of the wall neared completion the opposition from without was intensified, and took on more subtle forms. The first we might characterize as *compromise*, with a desire to inflict hurt, in this case evidently mischief of a personal sort. The request that there should be a conference in some village on the plain of Ono seemed reasonable enough then. In our day such a conference would have a special appeal, for all over the world nations and even tribes are full of disputes, and conferences continually take place, in order that, by some measure of compromise on both sides, open conflict may be avoided. Present-day statesmen would be very sympathetic to the suggestion of Sanballat and his friends.

But, when the truth of God or the work of God is in question, compromise is not to be entertained. The servant of God today may not fear physical mischief, but he knows that what is of *God* is not subject to human arrangement, however plausible such a compromise may appear to be.

The adversaries were persistent for they sent four times, and even a fifth, when they altered their tactics and resorted to *lying misrepresentation.* They accused him of desiring to throw off the Persian yoke and make himself a king. Similar tactics were employed by adversaries in the early days of the Gospel. Paul, for instance, was accused of being, 'a mover of sedition among all the Jews throughout the world' (Acts 24:5); and even in our day quite untrue charges have been levelled against preachers of the Gospel. These untrue charges against Nehemiah occasioned fear, though they knew them to be untrue, but in verse 9 we see that they only cast him afresh upon God. If opposition today casts us upon God, we shall ultimately profit thereby.

Verses 10-13, show us that the adversaries tried a third device, perhaps more crafty and subtle than the earlier ones. They hired a Jew, one of Nehemiah's own people, to alarm him as to his own danger of assassination, urging him to protect himself by doing something which would have been reprehensible according to his own religion. Not being one of the priests, to enter the temple and hide there was not permissible for him. If compromise and false accusation had not succeeded in moving him, they hoped to accomplish it by entrapping him in **A Sin Against the Law of His God.** But perceiving their wickedness, and calling again upon his God, this snare too was avoided by this God-fearing man.

How often have many of us, who seek to serve the Lord in this our day, been entrapped in somewhat similar fashion when opposed, committing ourselves in spirit, in word, in action to what is really sin against Him. If we would be delivered from entanglement in any of these three ways, let us keep in touch with God, as we see Nehemiah doing in this chapter. There is every reason for us to do so, since on the basis of His death and resurrection we are brought into such near and loving relationship with Him.

We must note verse 14, for it records the distressing fact that certain men who were prophets among the people, and even a prophetess, were in league with the adversaries and acting with them. Enemies of God's work, of a more secret sort, and even amongst the professed people of God, are really more dangerous to the work of God than opponents of an open sort. God, however, was behind the work on the wall, and so it was duly finished, as verses 15 and 16 record, in spite of all the antagonism and craft employed against the work, so that the enemies were cast down, seeing that God was in it.

The closing verses of the chapter again emphasize what appears to have been the main difficulty. Betrayal on the part of leaders within was worse than opposition from without. And, what led to this state of affairs? Marriage alliances with the enemy had taken place on the part of some, and the wish to smooth matters over was consequently very natural on the part of the transgressors. Ever since God said to Abram, 'Get thee out' (Genesis 12:1), these forbidden marriages had been a great snare. We have sadly to confess that it has not been otherwise in the history of the church.

As we read Paul's first epistle to the Corinthians, we might marvel at the number and variety of the disorders he had to refer to, and utter rebuke. What was the underlying cause? We believe this is reached in his second epistle, 6:11-18. At this point the Apostle's heart was enlarged and his mouth opened to indicate with plainness the weak spot. It was the way in which they had accepted the 'unequal', or 'diverse', yoke with unbelievers. The believer, born of God, has a nature which the unbeliever does not possess. At the same time he has within him the flesh, the old nature, which the unbeliever possesses. Hence if the diverse yoke be accepted, the believer is almost certain to be pulled in the direction of the world, and adopt some, if not many, of its ways. So let us today watch our ways, in the light of this plain New Testament scripture, lest we are guilty of a sin, which is similar to that which troubled Nehemiah in his day.

CHAPTER SEVEN

We have a sense of relief as we commence chapter 7, since we at once discover that there were those, who far from hindering the work of God at that moment, were real helpers in the work. The wall was finished, in spite of the difficulties, the doors set up and officials appointed, that the gates might be opened and shut as would be suitable. In this connection Hanani, whom Nehemiah calls 'my brother', is again mentioned. He it was who brought the first tidings of the sad state of the city and the Jews, as narrated in chapter 1:2. He is linked here with Hananiah, a ruler in the city, who is characterized as 'a faithful man', who 'feared God above many'. Since 'the fear of the Lord is the beginning of knowledge' (Proverbs 1:7), we may be sure that this man since he had progressed above many in it, had developed wise knowledge in a substantial measure. To have had such men, identifying themselves with him in his service, must have been an encouragement, granted to him by God. Such encouragement he needed for, as verse 4 records, the city was large, the people few, and though the wall was complete the houses were not as yet built.

Israel being God's earthly people, their genealogies were of importance and had to be carefully preserved. God having stirred the heart of Nehemiah on this matter, he found that a careful register had been made years before, when the first migration took place, as recorded at the beginning of the book of Ezra, and in view of its importance we have the register again recorded. Ezra 2:1-67, is repeated almost word for word in our chapter, verses 6-69. Then the four verses that close our chapter concerning the gifts of the chief of the fathers and of the people more generally, do differ from the record of the closing verses of Ezra 2. The much larger gifts recorded here are accounted for, we presume, by later gifts that had accrued up to Nehemiah's time. The title 'Tirshatha' applied to Nehemiah as well as to Zerubbabel. The gifts were large, and the priests and people were in their cities.

Then, as the last verse of the chapter tells us, came the seventh month.

CHAPTER EIGHT

Chapter 8 opens with the record of how the people were gathered together in the street before the water gate. Ezra the priest had been in Jerusalem for a number of years, but he now was called upon to bring the book of the law of the Lord and read it publicly before both men and women, and indeed before all who could understand it, which must have meant even children of maturer years. The word of God concerns everybody who has a mind capable of understanding it.

This public reading was a great occasion, and it furnishes us with some valuable instruction, particularly for those who minister the word in a public way. Ezra stood upon a pulpit, so that both he and the book out of which he read, were in full view of the people, and others helped to make the meaning plain to all who listened. If any of our readers engage in the public preaching of the Gospel or the ministry of the word to believers, we would ask them to read verse 8, and carefully note three words in it.

In the first place the book was read *distinctly*. What was written in the one precious book was clearly to reach the ears of the people, for they had no copies of it in their hands, which would enable them to check any mumbled or indistinct utterance. Secondly, they gave the *sense*, for during a thousand years the language may have altered somewhat, and many may have spoken the Aramaic and been unlearned in the ancient Hebrew. Thirdly, they made certain that the hearers really did *understand* the reading. How remarkably this verse anticipates the instructions given in 1 Corinthians 14, in regard to what is uttered in the Christian assembly. He who gives thanks, or prays, or ministers the word, is to make sure, not only that he himself really knows what he is saying, but that also he says it in such a way that it is understood, and therefore can be assimilated, and endorsed by the saying of 'Amen', by those who hear him. The speaker may say, 'I understood quite well what I wanted to convey.' We, however, have to reply, 'Yes, but did you speak with sufficient distinctness and simplicity, that your hearers got the sense and with clear understanding grasped your message?' A reference to our *understanding* occurs eight times in 1 Corinthians 14:9-20.

The first effect upon the people of this reading is revealed in verse 9—the people were moved to tears; and well they might be, for no one can face the demands of God's holy law without a sense of condemnation entering the conscience. Both Nehemiah and Ezra however stilled the people and bade them rejoice, for in the book there were of course the promises of God, showing mercy and predicting the Messiah, and further the Feast of Tabernacles was at hand, which was intended to be a season of happiness. They were entitled, of course, to rejoice in all that God had wrought on their behalf in spite of all the efforts of their adversaries. But we have wondered whether this switching of the emotions of the people from conviction and sorrow to eating and drinking and making 'great mirth', because they had understood, was really of God. Conviction of conscience is not easily reached, and consequently repentance is shallow all too often, though it is true of course that 'the joy of the Lord' imparts strength. There is however a great difference between that joy and making great mirth as one eats and drinks. The day will declare whether this successful direction of the leaders was really of God or not.

There was however on the part of the leaders a real desire to read and understand the directions of the law, as verse 13 records, and the original directions as to the feast of Tabernacles came clearly before them. This resulted in taking action to observe the feast as it had been written. The statement of verse 17, that this feast had not been so observed since the days of Joshua, might fill us with astonishment did we not know how easily and swiftly a decline from the instructions of the word of God can take place. When King Josiah moved the people in his day to keep the Passover, the record is that, 'there was no passover like to that kept in Israel from the days of Samuel the prophet' (2 Chronicles 35:18). This was an earlier exhibition of the same tendency, though not quite so extreme a case.

And what has taken place in the sad history of the professing church? We cannot, in this connection, throw stones at the people of Israel. In 1 Corinthians, chapters 12–14, we have revealed the great facts that govern the life and activities of the church as the body of Christ, followed by the commandments of the Lord, to be obeyed in the exercise of spiritual gifts, so that all may profit. For how long were they remembered and obeyed? Not for long. Soon other arrangements were made, which led in the course of a few centuries to the fearful evils of the Papacy, and what are called the 'Dark Ages'. There was possibly some remembrance of the word of God amongst the humble, unknown, persecuted saints, whom the Popes branded as 'heretics', but that was all, as many centuries passed. So we are not surprised at what is recorded in verse 17 of our chapter.

In the last verse of our chapter and the opening verses of chapter 9, we see that this reading of the book of the law, which started when Ezra mounted the pulpit, did not end there. It continued through the seven days of the feast, and even beyond. It lay at the root of such measure of revival as occurred at that time, and thus, we believe, it has always been. The revival that came to a head in the sixteenth century, sprang largely from the fact that the Scriptures had begun to be translated out of dead languages into languages that were alive, coupled with the invention of printing, that enabled countless thousands to read them. And so it has been again and again since that time.

CHAPTERS NINE AND TEN

In verses 2 and 3, we see the effect which the reading of the law had upon the hearers. Firstly, they *separated* themselves from all the entanglements with 'strangers', or 'foreigners', that they had been permitting. Secondly, they *confessed* their own sins, as well as the iniquities in which their fathers had been involved. Then thirdly, they honoured their God, by *worshipping* Him. They recognized that the word of the Lord, which they read, demanded obedience.

And this indeed is what we have to recognize. It is worthy of note that the epistle to the Romans, which, in its opening verses calls for *obedience* to the Gospel when it is preached, ends with the assertion that the 'mystery', which concerns Christ and the church, equally calls for 'the *obedience* of faith'. All the truth of God is revealed, not to provide us with philosophical ideas for the entertainment of our minds, but rather while entering mind and conscience, to lead us into happy obedience, as those brought into subjection to the will of God. This will certainly lead us into a life of separation from all that entangles and defiles, and also confession of failure and sin.

These two things must accompany each other. To separate without confession is not acceptable to God: neither is it acceptable if we confess without separating. When both are combined we are humbled before God, and brought into that state of mind and soul which befits us to take up our happy place as *worshippers* in the presence of God.

The worship that was offered to God through certain of the Levites is recounted in verses 4-6, of chapter 9. They confessed Jehovah as their God, and owned that He is the great Creator of heaven and earth, and exalted above all earthly and heavenly praise. It was suited to the revelation of God, in the light of which they lived. If we read Ephesians 1:3-7, we find the Apostle uttering worship in the light of the revelation that has reached us in Christ. And if we read Romans 11:33-36, we find the same Apostle in the spirit of worship as he contemplated the end to which His dealings with Israel will bring them, as well as ourselves. The Levites of Nehemiah's day could not anticipate the things made known to us, 'upon whom the ends of the ages are come' (1 Corinthians 10:11, New Trans.).

Having owned the Lord, as they knew Him at that time, they proceeded to recite before Him the wonder of His dealings with their nation, from Abram onwards through the centuries. The chapter is a lengthy one, and if it be carefully read, their chequered history comes before us, and we cannot fail to be struck by three things. First, *they vindicate God* in all His disciplinary dealings with them, as well as acknowledge His mighty power, that had wrought on their behalf in their deliverance from Egypt, their sustainment in the wilderness and their possession of the promised land. In all His dealings, God had acted towards them according to both mercy and righteousness.

And, in the second place, owning that the law with its 'right judgments', and 'good statutes', was perfect in its place, they made no attempt to justify their ancestors or themselves in their repeated sins and failures. *They condemned themselves* for their disobedience, which went even to the length of slaying the prophets, by whom God had testified against them and maintained His truth; and they owned the rightness of all that had come upon them, so that, though back in the land, they were still in a position of servitude to kings who were over them. This humble confession of sin was indeed good, equally with the acknowledgement of the rightness of all God's dealings with them.

But there was a third thing, which comes to light in the last verse of the chapter. Owning the 'great distress', that was still their portion, indeed because of it, they proposed to renew the old covenant of law, established originally with their ancestors, by making what they called 'a sure covenant', which they would write, and to which they would put their 'seal'.

So evidently they had not yet learned what the Apostle Paul so forcibly set before the Galatians— 'As many as are of the works of the law are *under the curse*' (3:10). The full period of Man's probation had not yet expired. Israel was the nation chosen of God in whom that probation, or testing, was to take place, and it did not end until they had crucified their Messiah. So we are not blaming these God-fearing Israelites for again making a covenant on the original lines of the law, and putting their seal to it, in the hope that they would succeed better than their fathers in keeping it.

We shall do well to note, however, what transpired in their later history. We shall not conclude our reading of this book without finding grievous failure recorded: and if we pass on to the book of the prophet Malachi, written perhaps half a century after this time, we find that a most deplorable state of things had developed amongst their children and descendants. There was still a certain amount of outward religious profession, while the law itself was broken, the whole spirit of it perverted, and the transgressors themselves completely self-satisfied and intolerant of criticism: so much so, that they repudiate with indignation any accusation that the prophet had to bring against them in the name of the Lord.

There was, however, a spirit of revival, clearly at work among the people, and since their place and standing before God was on the basis of the law of Moses, some fresh resolution to reverence and obey it was the appropriate thing they had to offer. There have been moments of revival in the history of the church, graciously granted by God, but what has marked them has been some fresh recovery, not of what we ought to do for God, but of *what He has done for us*—some fresh understanding and realization of the fulness of the grace into which we have been brought by the Gospel, and to the place of favour and heavenly relationship which is the church's portion, according to the eternal counsels and purposes of God.

In this long prayer of confession, as they reviewed the history of their nation, we find that twice they acknowledged one of the great root causes of their sin: their forefathers had, 'dealt proudly' (verses 16 and 29). Out of this spirit of pride, helped on doubtless by the very privilege and favour in which they stood as a nation, sprang the self-assertion and disobedience that had characterized their whole history; and that in their early days came to a head in the fact that they 'appointed a *captain* to return to their bondage' (verse 17), and when they 'made them a molten *calf* and said, This is thy God' (verse 18).

As a matter of history, the calf preceded the captain, for it was made at Sinai, when Moses was for so long on the mountain, as recorded in Exodus 32; whereas the proposal to appoint a captain and return to Egypt was made when they were condemned to 40 years wandering in the wilderness after the bad report of the spies, as recorded in Numbers 14. In reversing the historic order, it would seem that they first mentioned the *effect*, and then went back to the underlying *cause*.

The inspired comment on all this is, 'So we see that they could not enter in because of *unbelief*' (Hebrews 3:19). Unbelief wants a God plainly visible to the natural eye: hence the making of the calf. It also is not prepared to face a 40-year sojourn in a wilderness without visible resources: hence the desire for a captain after their own heart, to lead them back to a land of plenty, even if it be a land of slavery. It is easy for us to see their error, but let us not forget that the flesh in ourselves has exactly the same desires and tendencies. It longs for something visible, and for what panders to our natural desires, even if we are spiritually enslaved in obtaining it. Here is indeed a case in which the Old Testament Scriptures, which Timothy had known from a child, are able to make us *'wise unto salvation'* (2 Timothy 3:15).

We cannot indeed avoid the impression that similar evil principles were at work in the early centuries of the professing church. As faith vanished or declined, they wanted some visible representation of the Saviour, and then of His virgin mother. They wanted too a visible leader, who would relieve them of the troubles connected with the life of a stranger and a pilgrim in this present evil world, to which the Christian is called. As the centuries passed they got what they wanted in the crucifixes and images, and in the Papal chair, and its occupants, in Rome, that led them back into the spiritual bondage and darkness, of which Egypt was a type.

So the covenant was signed, which evidently reaffirmed their adherence to the old covenant, given at Sinai, which was indeed 'sure', in an absolute sense. They spoke of the covenant that they wrote and signed, as being sure, and so it was on God's side; but not so sure on their side, as we have already remarked. The first 27 verses of chapter 10, record the names of the leaders, who signed the covenant on behalf of the people; and then the rest of that chapter records how the people generally bound themselves to observe the law as to questions of marriage, and of ordinances concerning the upkeep of the temple service, and of the priests and Levites. They had separated themselves to obey the law, and as it says, they 'entered into a curse'. Everyone who stands before God on the basis of law, enters into a curse. Significantly enough, the last word in the Old Testament is the word 'curse'.

CHAPTER ELEVEN

The two verses that open chapter 11 may perhaps surprise us. We might have thought that, Jerusalem now being a walled city, there would have been strong competition among the people for the privilege of dwelling in it, but evidently it was not so. On the contrary, the country towns of Judah were more attractive, and therefore lots were cast, and one in ten of the people, on whom the lot fell, had to dwell in the city and if any offered themselves willingly to dwell there, the people blessed them, as though they made a sacrifice in so doing. The rest of the chapter puts on record the names of those who did dwell there, and also gives some details of their positions and the services they rendered. Their names may mean little to us, but may be important in the coming day of Israel's restoration and blessing.

What we may learn from it is surely this, that any sacrifice made, or service rendered, for God's work and interests is not forgotten but rather recorded before Him. The names of those who did not dwell in Jerusalem, but had more pleasure in the other places, are forgotten. Malachi tells us that in his day, 'a book of remembrance was written' before the Lord, 'for them that feared the Lord, and that thought upon His name'. That book was not peculiar to Malachi's day. It existed in Nehemiah's day, and exists in our day too. Let us not forget that!

CHAPTER TWELVE

The first 26 verses are occupied with further genealogical records, going back to the days of Zerubbabel and Jeshua the high priest. In verse 10, we learn that a grandson of Jeshua was Eliashib, who presently became high priest, and who had a son named, Joiada. These two are again mentioned in verse 22, and more concerning them appears in chapter 13.

In the remaining verses of the chapter, though many names are mentioned, it is not a matter of genealogy but rather of the part they had in the celebration of God's mercy at the solemn dedication of the wall that had now been completed. On this joyous occasion those who dwelt outside Jerusalem were assembled, as well as those living within it. One thing, however, was necessary: a purification had to take place, not only of priests and Levites, but also of the people and the gates and the wall itself. This we learn in verse 30.

The lesson this has for us is obvious. We may state it in few words—No *dedication* without *purification*. We are not told how this cleansing was effected, but it was of course done in some outward and visible fashion, which after all is but the figure and shadow of that inward work of which David had some understanding, as we see in Psalm 51:2, and again in Psalm 119:9. To dedicate is to devote to God and to His service: the force of the word is very similar to the apostolic injunction, 'present your bodies a living sacrifice' (Romans 12:1). We, as redeemed, are not our own, and God claims our very bodies to be devoted to Him and His service.

If now we turn to the verse just quoted, we find the very next words to 'sacrifice' are, '*holy*, acceptable unto God'. So here we are confronted by the same fact, what is dedicated to God must be cleansed and holy; that is, separated from defilement unto Him. The first eight chapters of Romans unfold the Gospel, in all its wonderful details, and by that Gospel we are justified and cleansed, and set apart for God.

The purification effected, the dedication was marked by three things. First, there was thanksgiving, and songs of praise to God. Second, there was great joy amongst the people, as they sacrificed, so that 'the joy of Jerusalem was heard even afar off'. Third, there was the bringing in of 'the offerings, for the firstfruits, and for the tithes'. Here again, we can see an analogy: if true dedication marks us, God will receive His portion in praise and thanksgiving; we shall have joy of heart; there will be no lack of gifts for the support of the work of God and of His servants. How do we stand in relation to these things?

CHAPTER THIRTEEN

In spite of these good features marking the dedication of the wall, things were not perfect. On that day they again read in the 'book of Moses', and found what had been written concerning their separation from the Ammonite and Moabite, in Deuteronomy 23. This led to a fresh concern as to the way they had failed in obedience, and a fresh separation from 'the mixed multitude', and further discovery of how, amongst leaders in their very midst, this instruction had been ignored.

Eliashib, mentioned in verse 4, was, as we have seen, a grandson of Jeshua the high priest, and was himself the high priest, as stated in verse 28 of this last chapter. So here, in what we may call the headquarters of their religion, was a flagrant violation of their law, for he had entered into alliance with Tobiah, one of the chief opponents of the work of God, and had prepared him a chamber in the precincts of the temple, just where the offerings and other treasures were stored. His dwelling there is even described as 'a great chamber'. If the visible head of their religious system thus transgressed, what could be expected of the common people?

How this came to pass is explained to us in verse 6. Twelve years had now passed since Nehemiah came to

Jerusalem with authority to rebuild the city, and he had gone back to Artaxerxes, who had made him the civil governor; hence he was absent from Jerusalem for some time. Having, however, obtained leave of the king to go back, this was the situation that confronted him. It grieved him much and he acted at once, casting out Tobiah's stuff, cleansing the chamber, and restoring it to its proper use. But what a tragedy was this! Here was a man, who was no priest, having to rebuke and reverse the action of the man, who was 'the high priest'! This tragedy has, sad to say, often been repeated in the history of the church. There is no guarantee of purity and of obedience to the will of God in *officialism*. Again and again God has raised up men in low office, or even outside office altogether, to bring about some revival of obedience to His revealed will.

Nehemiah having returned, this incident as to Eliashib evidently stirred him to investigate other matters, and the rest of the chapter gives in detail the painful discoveries that he made. These wrongs and departures from the law are grouped under three main heads. There was first, slackness in providing for the upkeep of the Levites and the singers, and the upkeep of the house of God generally. The people did not want the expense and bother of bringing in their tithes in regular fashion. Second, there were grave and open infractions of the law regarding the sabbath. The people were breaking it themselves and permitting 'men of Tyre' and others to trade with them, even in Jerusalem itself: very convenient, no doubt; but flagrantly breaking the law. Then third, there was this repeated tendency to marry heathen wives asserting itself, so soon after a reformation on this point. And this time even more flagrant, for 'wives of Ashdod', a Philistine city, were in question as well as of Ammon and Moab.

In this last sin the priestly family was again prominent, as we see in verse 28. The unnamed son of Joiada, grandson of Eliashib, was a great-great-grandson of that Jeshua the high priest, concerning whom Zechariah the prophet had the remarkable vision, which he recorded in chapter 3 of his prophecy. If that chapter be read, we see that a promise was made to him, 'if thou wilt walk in My ways, and if thou wilt keep My charge'. Whatever the said Joshua (or, Jeshua) did, it is very certain that his descendants and successors neither walked in the ways of God, nor kept His charge. Nehemiah saw this and as to this son of Joiada, he 'chased him from me'.

We may learn the further lesson that departure from the will and way of God is what we may call, *an infectious matter*. The chapter begins with Eliashib striking up an alliance with Tobiah the Ammonite and it ends with his grandson making an even more intimate alliance, by marriage, to a daughter of Sanballat the Horonite, who was an even more prominent adversary; since Tobiah is introduced as 'the servant', in chapter 2:10. If departure from God and His word starts as only a trickle, it may soon become a *torrent*. May this also have the effect of making us 'wise unto salvation'.

Finally let us observe that just as Nehemiah has to record the three grave departures that brought him into violent conflict with many, as he rectified what was wrong, so three times does he call upon God to remember him for good, according to the greatness of His mercy. He did indeed speak of his 'good deeds', yet acknowledge that he relied upon 'mercy' rather than reward. See verses 14, 22, 31.

Our first impression might be that he was somewhat self-centred, or self-satisfied: but our second thought would rather be, that he was acutely conscious that his strong action to maintain the law of God had brought him into unpopularity and under censure from many. The martyr Stephen said. 'Which of the prophets have not your fathers persecuted?' (Acts 7:52). They had persecuted them all, and Nehemiah, though not a prophet, uttering words of censure, had committed many acts of censure, which would have brought on his head more obloquy than words would ever have done.

Nehemiah's whole commission from God involved controversy, not only from without, but also, and perhaps more bitterly, from within. He was conscious that, if remembered for good of his God, all earthly disparagement would count for little.

Does faithfulness to God involve us today in condemnation from the world, or even worldly believers? Let us then, only aim at being remembered for 'good', when we stand before the judgment seat of Christ.

Haggai

INTRODUCTION

When considering the 4th and 5th chapters of the book of Ezra, we saw how the adversaries of God and of the remnant, who had returned to Jerusalem under Zerubbabel and Jeshua, and started to rebuild the temple, succeeded in stopping the work; and that God raised up two prophets, Haggai and Zechariah, under whose ministry the work was restarted. Turning now to the book of Haggai, we may find instruction in what God said through him.

His prophecy is carefully dated, and noting this we see it divides into four sections, though all were uttered in the second year of Darius. The first utterance was on the first day of the sixth month (1:1): the second on the twenty-first day of the seventh month (2:1): the third on the twenty-fourth day of the ninth month (2:10): the fourth, though distinct from the third, was given on the very same day (2:20). Our first remark must be that God always recognizes the validity of His own governmental actions. He had set Israel aside as a nation, and the times of the Gentiles had begun; hence the dating is that of the ruling Gentile power and not that of the Jews.

Has this point any significance for us? We believe it has. We live, as we believe, near the end of the sad history of the Church as a professing body on the earth, subject to God's holy government. Some idea of that government may be ours if we consider with care Revelation 2 and 3, where the Lord as a Judge surveys the seven churches, and speaks of such things as the removal of the 'candlestick' of light and testimony, and acting so as to 'fight against' the evil doers; and even when there is a measure of approval, it is only 'a little strength' and the minimum of faithfulness.

We shall do well if we remember this with much humility of mind. The overcomers in the seven churches are not exempted from the painful results of God's government, but must overcome in the conditions that prevail. The Apostle Peter had to say, 'the time is come that judgment must begin at the house of God'; and nineteen centuries have passed since that was written. Here is a fact that bears upon much painful weakness that confronts us today.

Because of the weakness marking the returned remnant, God raised up Haggai. Because of the contrary edict of the new Persian king they had stopped the work on the house of God, and evidently without much concern they had started to build nice and comfortable houses for themselves. This being the case the prophet's first utterance was *a word of rebuke*.

CHAPTER ONE

The people adopted a fatalistic attitude, saying, 'the time is not come ... that the *Lord's* house should be built'; and started to build up their own affairs. Some sixty years ago we heard Christians saying, in spite of the Lord's words in Acts 1:8, that the time for the evangelization of the distant heathen was not come, and they settled down to build up their own spiritual affairs, as they considered them to be. It was not wrong for these Jews to build themselves some houses, but it was wrong for them to settle down to this and let the house of God lie waste, hence the drought, and God did 'blow upon' all their efforts.

It is not wrong for us today to care for our own spiritual state; indeed we are admonished, 'building up yourselves on your most holy faith' (Jude 20), but as the succeeding verses show, this is to be done as the fruit of the love of God, which expresses itself in 'compassion' upon some, and as to others saving them with fear. We are not to concentrate upon ourselves to the exclusion of God's work and God's interests today. The word of our Lord still stands, 'Seek ye first the kingdom of God and His righteousness; and all these things shall be added unto you'.

Do we modern Christians require a word of rebuke, because we neglect God's interests in favour of our own interests? We fear that all too often we do. Let us accept the rebuke with the humility of mind that becomes us.

This is what the people did, led by Zerubbabel and Joshua, and they set to work in obedience to the word of the Lord. Haggai was to them the Lord's messenger, bringing them the Lord's message, and he gave them the assurance that God Himself was with them in the prosecution of the work. It was so pleasing to God, that the very day they recommenced the work is placed on record in the last verse of the chapter; exactly twenty-three days after the word of rebuke had reached them.

The assuring word from the Lord, 'I am with you', really settled everything. The Apostle could write, 'If God be for us, who can be against us?' and this, though stated in New Testament days, was just as true in earlier days. The people soon discovered that difficulties vanished when God was with them, as the book of Ezra has shown us. Their adversaries sprang to life directly the work recommenced, and reported their activity to headquarters, but another king was now on the throne in Persia, who rescinded the decree of Artaxerxes, and restored the original decree of Cyrus, under which the remnant had returned. So once more the voice of the Lord was being obeyed: and obedience is ever the way to blessing.

CHAPTER TWO

Hence about four weeks later there came another message from the Lord through the prophet Haggai, and this time it was *a word of encouragement*. It was specially addressed to the very old people, who might have some recollection of the magnificence of Solomon's temple, and consequently realize how inferior was any temple that they could hope to raise. The encouragement ministered was twofold. It had first a present aspect and then a future one.

But first let us note how this record bears upon ourselves today. There has been, in the history of the professing church some recovery of truth and some reversion to the simplicity of things, as ordered of God by His Spirit at the beginning, analogous to this return of a remnant to the place where God had placed His name, and had His house long before. The devoted saints of God, who had some part in this recovery, must surely have been conscious that anything of an outward nature into which they came, was far below the greatness of that which was established visibly on the Day of Pentecost, when three thousand were converted, and 'continued stedfastly in the apostles' doctrine, and fellowship, and in breaking of bread, and in prayers' (Acts 2:42). It would indeed be good if we today were fully conscious of the smallness and feebleness of all that is in our hands, if compared with the greatness of that which originally was instituted of God.

And if we are duly impressed with this fact, and therefore liable to be somewhat depressed by the contrast we observe, we may be cheered as we discover how the word of encouragement ministered through Haggai, has a remarkable application to ourselves.

The encouragement in its present aspect we find in verses 4 and 5. Not only did God pledge His presence with them, but He added, 'The word that I covenanted with you when ye came out of Egypt, and My Spirit, remain among you: fear ye not' (New Trans.). He cast them back upon the integrity of the word to direct their ways, which He gave at the beginning of His dealings with them, and the guidance and power of His Spirit, who was still among them. If we were asked what are the resources still available for saints today, we should have to answer that we still have the authentic word of God, dating, 'from the beginning', as the Apostle John so frequently reminds us in his epistles; and then that the Holy Spirit, who was shed forth on the Day of Pentecost, still indwells the saints, and therefore, if ungrieved, His power is still available for us. So we too need not fear, though opponents are many and difficulties persist.

As to the future there was also a word of encouragement though a time of judgment was to come. The very earth on which man lives, together with the heavens that envelop it, are to be shaken, as well as all the nations that inhabit it. The instability of themselves, and of all that surrounded them, had to be feared by the Jews of that day. And we have to face it also for as we reach the end of Hebrews 12, we find these words of Haggai quoted as applying to the end of the age. His words, 'Yet once', are quoted as, 'Yet once more', and therefore as applying to such a final removing of every shakeable thing, that it never needs to be repeated.

And when that great shaking takes place, 'the desire of all nations' will come and the house of God be filled with glory. Now Christ personally can hardly be spoken of as the *'desire'* of all nations, since when He shall appear in glory, so that every eye sees Him, 'all kindreds of the earth shall *wail* because of Him' (Revelation 1:7). But though this is so, the nations have ever desired such peace and fruitfulness, such prosperity, and quietness and assurance for ever, as is predicted in Isaiah 32:15-18. These very desirable things will only come to pass and be enjoyed when the Lord Jesus comes again; and hence, we judge, this prophetic word does look on to the advent of Christ. When He comes, He will bring these blessings to men, and glory to the house of God.

The better translation of verse 9 appears to be, 'The latter glory of this house shall be greater than the former'. The house of God in Jerusalem is considered as one, though broken down and rebuilt on several occasions, and the glory of its final form will outshine even its first glory as built by Solomon, when visible glory filled the building; so much so that the priests could not enter. That final glory was seen in vision by

Ezekiel, as he records at the beginning of his 43rd chapter. We can thank God that the same thing will be true in regard to the church. Its latter end, when invested with the glory of Christ, will exceed all that marked it at the beginning.

One further item of encouragement was presented through Haggai— 'in this place will I give peace, saith the Lord of hosts'. Now we think it would be true to say that no city has had a more tempestuous history, and endured more sieges, than Jerusalem; indeed even today we hear Palestine spoken of as 'the cockpit of the nations'; and so indeed it is going to be, as Zechariah 14:2 declares; yet the place of peace it will ultimately prove to be.

Now let us carefully note that all this blessing, glory and peace, to be reached after the predicted mighty shaking, is not going to be reached as the result of human effort or the fruit of human faithfulness, for it is God declaring what He will bring to pass as the fruit of His sovereign mercy. The returned remnant had now responded to the word of rebuke and set their faces in the right direction, and what greater encouragement than for God to tell them, while still in felt weakness, what He proposed ultimately to bring to pass.

It is even so with us today. We are in weakness—and happy are we if it is *felt* weakness—but if our hearts are set in the right direction, seeking the furtherance of God's present work in grace, we may find great encouragement and joy as we consider the New Testament predictions as to the future glory of the church in association with Christ, reached according to God's sovereign purpose. We look, as Jude tells us in his epistle, for 'mercy of our Lord Jesus Christ unto eternal life'. We shall reach glory, not as the fruit of *our merit*, but of *His mercy*.

A little more than two months passed and then the Lord saw that the people, now busy in His work, needed another message and this time *a word of warning*. It was addressed more particularly to the priests though it concerned the work of all the people. Two questions were raised with them concerning their work: one recorded in verse 12, and the reverse question in verse 13. The priests had to admit that what is unclean and unholy is infectious and therefore defiling, what is holy and clean is not transmitted in the same way. Here is a matter of much importance from a spiritual standpoint.

The principle is illustrated even in natural things. Everyone knows that if a rotten apple is placed in a box of good ones, the rottenness will soon spread; whereas no one imagines that rotten apples will be made good by placing a few sound ones among them. In the temple service this matter had to be observed, and like all these outward observances under the law, the point has an inward and spiritual instruction for us. Let us heed it, since we have the defiling 'flesh' within as well as the defiling 'world' without.

The application that Haggai had to make of these questions was calculated to have a searching and sobering effect upon the people. Stirred up, as they had been, to put their hands to the work of building the house, there would have been a tendency towards self-complacency as though all was as it should be. They were plainly told it was not so, but that what was imperfect and unclean marked their best work. A humbling lesson for them—and for us also. If some little reviving is granted to us today in the mercy of God, how easily the defilements of the flesh creep in: how quickly we may become like the early Christians in Galatia, who though beginning 'in the Spirit', proceeded as though they might be 'made perfect by the flesh' (Galatians 3:3).

But having warned them as to the imperfection that marked their work, the prophet proceeded to assure them that in spite of it the blessing of God rested upon them. In contrast to the times of scarcity and blasting and mildew, that they had experienced while they neglected the house of God and set themselves to embellish their own houses, they now saw the hand of God working in their favour, giving them plenty of earth's good things. Thus it is today. There are elements of failure and uncleanness in all our service, but in spite of that, if the heart be right, we may expect spiritual blessing from God.

The frequent occurrence of the word, 'Consider', in this short prophecy is worthy of note. Twice in the first section did the prophet have to say to the people, 'Consider *your ways*'. And now in this later section the word occurs thrice—verses 15 and 18—and we find the prophet saying in effect, 'Consider *God's ways*'. He delights to own any measure of energy and faithfulness in His service, even though there is a measure of uncleanness and failure connected with it, and to respond to it in blessing. In our present feebleness, conscious of failure, proceeding both from the flesh within and the world without, we may take much comfort from this.

The last section begins with verse 20. We have had, what we have ventured to call, the word of rebuke, followed by the word of encouragement, and then the word of warning. We now have what we may call the *word of exaltation*, addressed personally to Zerubbabel, who was a prince of David's line, as stated in Matthew 1:12. The last verse of the chapter doubtless had some application to the man himself. Kingdoms would be overthrown, as predicted in Daniel 11, but he would be as a signet-ring, by which God would establish His decrees. How this worked out for Zerubbabel we know not, but we believe the Spirit of God had in view, not so much some temporary exaltation of this man, but the permanent exaltation of One whom he typified; even our Lord Jesus Christ.

Viewing it thus, we seem to have here an Old Testament forecast of what is more definitely stated when we read of our Lord that, 'All the promises of God in Him are Yea, and in Him Amen, unto the glory of God by us' (2 Corinthians 1:20). Only here of course the thought is greatly amplified. Christ is He who will not only set forth and establish, as under the stamp of a signet-ring, all God's purposes, expressed in His promises, but also carry them to their fulness and completion so that at last the great 'Amen' can be said. The Apostle Paul added the words 'by us', because he was dealing there with what God had promised for the saints today, such as ourselves.

So Haggai finishes with a prediction that points to the coming exaltation of the One whom we worship as our Saviour and our Lord. He does so in a typical and symbolic way, some centuries before His first advent in lowly humiliation. We wait for their fulfilment in a far more glorious way than Haggai can have known, when at His second advent He appears in great glory.

Zechariah

As we commence to read Zechariah we note that, just as with Haggai, definite dates are given for the messages that God gave through him; and the first verse reveals that his first message—verses 2-6—was uttered between Haggai's *word of encouragement*, in the early part of his second chapter, and the *word of warning*, recorded later in that chapter. We think we may term Zechariah's first message, *a word of exhortation*.

We may wonder perhaps, why such a word at that juncture was needed? Had the people not responded to the word of rebuke, and so diligently resumed work on the temple that they were encouraged by a prophetic view of its future glory? Yet before Haggai's word of warning, uttered on the ninth month there came this call to them to remember the directness and certainty of God's governmental dealings with their fathers, and the certainty of similar dealings if like their fathers, they turned away from Him. The exhortation therefore is, 'Turn ye unto Me, saith the Lord of hosts'. Had they not done this? Yes, indeed, *outwardly* and *in action*. But had there been that *inward* and *vital* turning of heart, which is what counts in the sight of God? Their subsequent history, as revealed by the prophet Malachi, shows how little they were marked by this inward turning of heart to God.

So, as we open this fresh prophecy, we meet with something calculated to make us 'wise unto salvation', from a similar danger today. How easy for us to be satisfied with correctness of outward behaviour, without that inward heart-turning, of great value in the sight of God. Very possibly the 'uncleanness', which in his third message Haggai pointed out as marring the work of their hands, was connected with this matter.

In verse 7 we travel on to the eleventh month of the second year of Darius, so important in the history of the Jews, and we commence a whole series of visions which were granted to the prophet—visions which had a bearing upon their position at that time, but which carried in them allusions to the far future, and the ultimate deliverance to come through Christ.

Before starting on them we may pause to notice the great difference of style that marked the two prophets. Of all the Minor prophets, none is more plain and direct, and free from figurative language and visions, than Haggai: and none more full of figurative language and the record of visions than Zechariah; yet both were equally used, and at the same time. We see foreshadowed that which comes plainly to light in God's administration for the Church, as recorded in 1 Corinthians 12–14. What God establishes is marked by *diversity* in *unity*. Each servant of God is marked by difference and variety as to detail—like the many differing members of the human body—but all bound together in a God-created unity. Let us never forget this fact in our dealings with, or our judgments of, God's many servants today.

From verse 7 of our first chapter, till the later part of chapter 6, we get a series of visions that were granted to the prophet, and recorded by him. The words, 'Then lifted I up mine eyes' (1:18), occur a number of times, as he puts on record what he saw. As we ponder these visions we may discern a certain sequence in them.

The first is that of the rider on a red horse among the myrtle trees, and behind him other horses, red, speckled and white. They represented those whom the Lord had sent forth to walk to and fro through the earth. As a symbol, a horse is generally used to indicate strength and power, but in this first vision nothing is said to show just what form of strength is meant, though we gather not earthly kingdoms, such as Persia or Greece, since the horses walk on tours of inspection through the earth. When, however, we read chapter 6, we again find horses mentioned, and they are described as, 'the four spirits of the heavens'; that is, they are angelic in character. This, we believe, they are here; and their report is that though God's city and people were still in distress at the end of the seventy years, the nations under the Persian empire were having a very quiet and restful time.

This being so, the angel of the Lord gave Zechariah a clear message to the effect that He was sore displeased with the apparently prosperous nations, and was going indeed to return to Jerusalem in blessing. Reading verses 16 and 17, we cannot but feel that though the help and blessing that visited the people during the next few years was a fulfilment of these words, the complete fulfilment awaits the time when the glorious appearing of Jehovah, predicted in Zechariah's last chapter, takes place.

Then a fresh vision met the eyes of the prophet: the four horns representing the four earthly powers that were permitted to scatter so completely the people and their city. Then there came into his view the four carpenters, who would come, as sent of God, to disturb and destroy the four powers that had done it. The prophecy views the whole matter in a comprehensive way, as from God's side. In Zechariah's days, the first of these 'horns', the Babylonian empire, had been 'cast out', and the second was in power, the third and fourth yet to come; but God was making known the fact that their rule was only temporary, and that each would be 'cast out' in turn.

There can be no doubt, we think, as to the identity of the four horns, though we may not be able to identify in the same way the four carpenters. We believe, however, again that the prophecy is not yet completely fulfilled, for the 'horns of the Gentiles', which lift up their power for the scattering of Israel, are not completely disposed of while 'the times of the Gentiles' (Luke 21:24) still run their course. But the remnant, now back in Jerusalem, were given the encouragement of knowing that the day of their oppressors would come to an end in God's own time. It is an encouragement to us to know it also.

Chapter Two

The adversaries being disposed of, the vision of chapter 2 carries the predictions a further step forward. That God should send a man with a line in his hand, wherewith to measure Jerusalem, indicated that the city was still an object of His attention and interest. The Jews that surrounded Zechariah might be pleased with the progress of their rebuilding operations, and inclined to be complacent about it, but they were to know that God had far more wonderful things in view, as the angel proceeds to explain.

A day is to come when Jerusalem would need no wall, such as the people would soon be building, for Jehovah Himself would be as a wall of fire round about and, even more wonderful, be Himself 'the glory in the midst of her'. Multitudes will be within her in that day, for there will be a great exodus from the lands of their scattering and particularly from 'the land of the north', as is revealed in verses 6-9. This migration will take place, as verse 8 indicates, 'after the glory' has been revealed and established. So that again we have to say that the prophecy goes far beyond anything that has yet transpired and looks on to the time of the end.

This is made yet more plain as we read the four verses that close this chapter. Never yet has Jehovah been dwelling in Zion, and inheriting Judah as His portion, with many nations 'joined to the Lord'. But that day will yet come to pass. At the present time God is not joining nations unto Himself, but rather He is visiting them, 'to take out of them a people for His name' (Acts 15:14).

CHAPTER THREE

A fourth vision is recorded in chapter 3, concerning Joshua the high priest, and the removal from him of all that was defiling. In verse 8, we read of him and his fellows that they were 'men wondered at', or, as Darby's New Translation puts it, 'men of portent', with the note, 'men to be observed as signs, or types'. Regarding Joshua therefore as a type, we see a plain prediction that it will only be as cleansed from their filth that the people will enjoy the blessing connected with the dwelling of Jehovah in Zion, as just foretold. There can be no nearness to God without deliverance from the filth of sin. No change of dispensation alters this fact.

It is worthy of note that Zechariah saw, not some erring and disreputable man clothed in filthy garments, but a man who had been used of God and in a place of special privilege. We are reminded that David exclaimed, 'Verily *every* man at his *best* state is *altogether* vanity' (Psalm 39:5). If Joshua needed cleansing from filth, then they all did. Now Satan was there to resist this cleansing, but he was rebuked since Joshua was 'a brand plucked out of the fire'. This vision supplements what Haggai had to say to the people, in his second chapter about their uncleannesses. But Joshua in this vision was not only delivered from his filthy garments, but was clothed in what was clean with a fair mitre upon his head. He was thus established in his priestly position. God does not only remove evil; He also crowns with good.

But all this will really be established when God brings forth His Servant 'the Branch' who had been predicted under this figure nearly a century before, as we see in Jeremiah 23:5-6, where the Branch is revealed to be 'Jehovah tsidkenu'—the Lord our righteousness. We have to travel back to old Jacob for the first reference to 'the stone of Israel' (Genesis 49:24). He is not only the One who will introduce and establish righteousness, but also the foundation stone, upon which will be built everything that is going to stand unshaken, for He who is the stone has complete power of perception, represented in the 'seven eyes', so that nothing unclean can ever creep in. So, in that day, as the last verse indicates, there will be quietness and assurance for ever.

Chapter Four

A fifth vision follows in chapter 4, which indicated, as we understand it, a further thing needful if the full blessing, revealed to the prophet, is to be securely established; namely, the energy of the Spirit of God. The prophet was shown a golden candlestick supplied with oil, after the fashion of the candlestick that had been in the tabernacle and the temple. On confessing his ignorance as to the meaning of this vision, he was instructed as to its present application. This time the vision concerned not Joshua the religious leader, but Zerubbabel the civil leader of the people, who might be tempted to fall back on purely human things to accomplish what he felt would be right. He is instructed that his resource lay not in 'might', or armed force; nor in 'power', or authority, derived from men, but in the Spirit of the Lord of hosts. Obstacles, like a great mountain, might rise before him, but all would be levelled and the 'headstone' be brought forth with rejoicing, and the cry of, 'Grace, Grace'.

Verses 8-10, show the application of all this to the immediate task before Zerubbabel. Relying not upon human force or power but upon God, he would be enabled to finish the work of rebuilding the house. It was, as compared with the days of Solomon, a day of small things, but not to be despised on account of that. In verse 10 the marginal reading is the better. The seven eyes of the Lord, seen in the previous chapter, 'upon one stone', shall rejoice, since they run to and fro through the whole earth, and everything is observed by them.

It is plain then that God gave encouragement through the prophet, and in connection with the two leaders of the people. The two things needed were cleansing as seen with Joshua, and spiritual power as shown to Zerubbabel. And in all this there lay an indication of how God will bring in the ultimate blessing at the end of the age.

The prophet now raises a question as to the meaning of the two olive trees that supplied the oil to the golden candlestick; the very oil itself being spoken of as 'the gold'. The answer was that they represented the two 'anointed ones', or 'sons of oil', that stand before 'the Lord of the whole earth'. In Israel the high priest was anointed, and also the king—David for instance, in 1 Samuel 16. At that moment Joshua represented the priestly line, and Zerubbabel, the kingly line, though not himself a king. The grace and power of God was to flow through them at that time, in its measure. In full measure it will flow through Christ, when He will sit a Priest upon His kingly throne, as the sixth chapter will tell us. It will then be perfectly clear that all is reached on the basis of grace, and not of law-keeping. Compared with the New Testament, the Old has but little to tell us of the grace of God, but here we have it emphasized. 'Grace, Grace', will indeed be the cry when all is established in the Messiah, anointed both as Priest and King.

CHAPTER FIVE

The other side of the picture meets us as we read chapter 5. In a sixth vision the prophet saw a flying 'roll'; symbolically representing the law, extending its authority over all the earth, and bringing with it a curse. The two sins specified—stealing and swearing—both exceedingly common, represent sin against man and against God. The fact that God acts in grace does not mean that there is any condonation of sin, on which the curse lies. And as Galatians 3:10 tells us, 'As many as are of the works of the law are under the curse'. A proper sense of this only enhances our wonder, and appreciation of the grace of God.

The second part of this vision reveals what had to take place in view of this curse. An ephah was the common measure of trade and commerce, and a woman is several times used in Scripture as a symbol of a system; and systemized idolatry, linked with profitable business had lain at the root of the evils that had led to the captivity out of which the remnant had come; and the land of Shinar, where Babylon was situated, had been the original home and hotbed of all idolatry. It was this that had brought the curse upon the forefathers of the people. The whole system of this idolatrous evil had to be deported to its own base.

Now this is what in figure seems to be depicted here. It was not so much a personal matter, as presented in the cleansing of Joshua in chapter 3, but a national cleansing from the sin of idolatry. This did come to pass historically, as we know, and from about that time the Jews have not turned aside to the idols of the nations. If Matthew 12:43-45, be read, we see how our Lord made reference to this act, and yet predicted how ultimately they will be dominated by this sin in an intensified form. But for the time being they were delivered.

CHAPTER SIX

The last of this series of visions meets us as we read the early part of chapter 6. Again, as in the first vision, four horses are seen, but this time in chariots and no riders are mentioned. Again there seems to be some connection with the four great world-empires, that successively follow during the time that Israel is set aside; yet they are stated to be, 'the four spirits of the heavens, which go forth from standing before the Lord of all the earth'. In the closing chapters of Daniel we are permitted to know that angelic beings hold commissions in connection with certain nations; Michael, for instance in connection with Israel. It is an obscure theme, but it seems to be alluded to here, and Zechariah is given to know that there was at that time quietness in the 'north country'; which would indicate that for some little time the Jews would be permitted to pursue their way in peace. We may be thankful that in our day, as in that day, the controlling hand of God is on and over the nations.

The series of visions being finished, Zechariah is directed to perform a striking symbolic act in the presence of certain men of the captivity, who were then present. Crowns, which are a symbol of royalty, were to be made, primarily for the head of Joshua the high priest, though also to be given as a memorial to the four men mentioned. In Zechariah 3 Joshua was *cleansed*, as representing the people, and then came the prediction as to the **Branch**, who would truly be Jehovah's Servant. Here, Joshua is *crowned*, inasmuch as for the moment he is made into a type of the **Branch**, who was to come.

When Zechariah had thus done as he was told, there was the high priest, crowned as a king. Thus was set forth the Coming One, who was to build the temple of the Lord. But were they not engaged in the building of a temple? They were: but they were thus notified that all they were building was provisional and not the final thing, when its latter glory would exceed its first glory, as they had been told through Haggai. The Branch, or, Sprout, of David's line would accomplish the permanent work, and He would be a King, as well as Priest, when He did it.

By the oath of Jehovah, according to Psalm 110, Christ is 'Priest for ever after the order of Melchizedek'. When at last in Zion the kingly crown rests upon His head, He will not relinquish His priestly service, but 'be a Priest upon His throne'. The two things, which so often among men have been in opposition, will be united harmoniously in Him. How often have kingly authority and priestly grace clashed amongst sinful men? They will not do so when this prophecy is fulfilled; for, 'the counsel of peace shall be between them both'.

In result, this further great prediction will be fulfilled— 'He shall bear the glory'. Glory in a small measure has before now descended upon human shoulders, that were unable to bear it, so speedily it vanished. At last it will descend upon One able and worthy to sustain it for ever. What a day that will be! Well may we anticipate it with joy.

CHAPTER SEVEN

In the first verse of chapter 7, we find another date given; almost two years later than that of the visions just recorded, and the prophecies of Haggai. These fresh prophecies were occasioned by the arrival of certain men with questions as to the observance of fasts, and we notice that we pass from the record of visions to a series of plain declarations of God's message. We now find repeated not, 'I lifted up mine eyes', but rather, 'The word of the Lord came'.

The question raised by these men concerned a fast in the fifth month, which had been observed for many years. From Jeremiah 52:12, we learn that it was in that month the Babylonian army had burned Solomon's magnificent temple, and wrecked Jerusalem. Now once more the house of the Lord was being built, if not entirely finished, so was it suitable that they should still observe the fast? A very natural question!

The answer of God through Zechariah linked with this fast another in the seventh month, which apparently was in memory of the murder of Gedaliah and others, and the flight of the remnant, left in the land, into Egypt, as recorded in 2 Kings 25:25-26. These tragedies were commemorated with fasting and tears, during the seventy years captivity. As far as we can discern, no direct answer was given to the question they raised: instead another question was raised with them. Did they have Jehovah before their minds in their observances or only themselves? And when the fast was over, did they return to their eating and drinking just enjoying themselves? Did they really fast, enquired the Lord, 'unto Me, even to Me?'

Here is deeply important instruction for ourselves. We may put it thus: *In our observances and service a right motive is everything.* We may diligently observe the Lord's Supper on the first day of the week, diligently preach the Gospel, or minister to the saints; but are we doing it with God Himself, revealed in Christ, before us, or are we just pursuing an agreeable ritual and maintaining our own reputations in it all? A searching question, which the writer had better ask himself as well as the readers ask themselves.

If the people had kept the Lord before them and observed His words through the former prophets, things would have been far otherwise. And what was His word now through Zechariah, but just what it had been through them. Take Isaiah's first chapter as an example. He accused the people of moral corruption, whilst maintaining ceremonial exactitude. In verses 11-14 of our chapter the men who enquired are reminded of this, and are plainly challenged as to the present attitude of themselves and the people of their day, as we see in verses 8-10. The moral evils that had wrecked the nation were still working amongst the people that had returned to the land. A remnant may return but the inveterate tendency to develop the old evils remains. Let us never forget that.

CHAPTER EIGHT

But having exposed the sinful state of the people, another word from the Lord came in which the purposes of His mercy were revealed, as we see in chapter 8. In this remarkable chapter there are things specially addressed to the remnant then back in the land—verses 9-17, for instance—yet the main drift of it goes far beyond anything that was realized in their history, between the rebuilding as permitted by Cyrus, and the destruction under the Romans; so it looks on to the end of the age and the second coming of Christ.

In that age Jerusalem will indeed have Jehovah dwelling in her midst and be called 'a city of truth'. Once indeed He who was the 'truth', as well as the 'way', and the 'life', was in her midst, only to be rejected and crucified, while Pilate, who sanctioned that act of rejection, asked satirically, 'What is truth?' No, Jerusalem has never yet been worthy of that designation; but she will be in a coming age. And then human life will be greatly prolonged, and young life be abundant and free. Our modern streets with fast-moving motor traffic are hardly a playground for children.

Verses 6-8, also look on to the time of the end. What had come to pass in the return of the remnant was indeed wonderful in their eyes, but what is here predicted would be more wonderful still, when God would gather from the west as well as the east, to dwell as His people, so that He would be their God 'in truth and in righteousness'. In Christ truth and righteousness have indeed been revealed and established, but never yet has God dwelt in Jerusalem on that basis. The day is coming when He will do so.

In verses 9-16, there is a special appeal to the remnant of the people then in the land. They are reminded of the words spoken to them earlier, when the foundation of the temple was laid, and how the adversity that had marked their doings had been turned into a time of prosperity. God was now bestowing much favour and prosperity upon them, but they are reminded that He called for suitable behaviour on their part. Truth, honesty and righteous judgment was what was expected of them. Again the stress is on the moral qualities that are according to God, and not on ceremonial observances.

A further word from the Lord is now given and in verse 19 four fasts are mentioned. Besides the two mentioned in the previous chapter we now have the one in the fourth month, for in that month famine prevailed and Jerusalem was broken up, according to Jeremiah 52:6-7, and it was in the tenth month that the city was surrounded by Nebuchadnezzar's army, as verse 4 of that same chapter records. It is now revealed that the day would come when these four fasts would be turned into feasts of rejoicing. Therefore they were to love truth and peace. These predictions of future blessing were to have a present effect upon the people.

And all that we know of future blessing should have a present effect of good upon ourselves. It is worthy of note that truth precedes peace, as cause and effect. Error produces strife just as certainly as truth produces peace. In the remaining verses of our chapter we find predictions of the happy state of things that will prevail when truth at last prevails in Jerusalem, and peace fills the scene. In that coming day the house of the Lord will indeed be, 'an house of prayer for all people' (Isaiah 56:7). There will be many who desire to seek the Lord in prayer, and they will recognize where God is to be found in that day. All through the centuries the name, 'Jew', has had a measure of reproach attaching to it. It will not be so then, for they will recognize that at last God is with His ancient people. It is obvious that this prediction has never yet been fulfilled, and looks on to a future day.

CHAPTER NINE

The word of the Lord that opens chapter 9 is spoken of as a 'burden', since it starts with solemn words of judgment on peoples that surrounded the land of Israel. Some of these judgments took place soon after the predictions were uttered; that upon Tyre, for instance, and upon the cities of the Philistines. Darby's New Translation tells us that an alternate rendering to 'bastard', is one 'of a foreign race'. But even so there will apparently be a remainder, or a remnant, who will be for God and belong to Him. Moreover, however powerful oppressors may appear to be, God will encamp about His house in protecting mercy. And how will this be brought to pass?

Verses 9 and 10 answer this question, for in these two verses the two advents of the Lord Jesus are brought before us. The coming of the King will settle everything, but we can imagine how the reader of Zechariah's day might pause at this ninth verse in amazement, feeling that in the presence of powerful outside foes, and the inward defection so plainly manifested amongst the Jews, some great and majestic and powerful Deliverer was needful, and the King is announced as lowly in His person and in His approach. True, He is to have salvation, but this was not the kind of King that was popularly expected.

The Spirit of God, who inspired this prophecy knew very well that there was a deeper question to be settled before there could be the intervention in power that was so ardently desired. First must come the bearing of the full penalty of human sin, and hence the Divinely reached settlement of that dreadful matter, and, that accomplished, there could be emancipation from sin's power. This had been set forth typically in Exodus 12 and 14. First the blood of the lambs in Egypt, and then deliverance by the overthrow of Egypt. The latter is more spectacular, but the former a far deeper thing.

In the Gospels we see how the more spectacular filled the minds of the disciples. Even when they acted and played their part in the fulfilment of verse 9, they did not realize they were doing it. This we are plainly told in John 12:16. Only when Jesus was glorified and the Holy Spirit was given did they realize the true significance of what they had done. Again, in Acts 1:6, we see how the coming of the kingdom in power filled their thoughts before the Spirit was given. The coming of the King in lowly grace was but little understood or anticipated by the great majority.

But the Messiah will come in power and have dominion over all the earth, as verse 10 declares. The way His widespread kingship is stated here agrees exactly with the inspired statement through David centuries before written in Psalm 72:8. When David foresaw this by the Spirit, every desire of his heart was satisfied, and he had nothing left to pray for, as the last verse of the psalm tells us. What our prophet tells us is that the days of warfare will be over—chariot and battle bow cut off, and peace imposed upon the nations.

Verse 11 appears to be a word specially addressed to the sons of Israel, for Ephraim is addressed in verse 13, as well as Judah. They have all been like prisoners, entrapped in a waterless pit, waiting and hoping for deliverance. When Messiah comes in power, deliverance will reach them but only through 'the blood of thy covenant'. Here we see an allusion to that new covenant of grace, predicted in Jeremiah 31:31, illuminated for us by the words of the Lord Jesus at the institution of His Supper, when He spoke of, 'My blood of the new testament' (Matthew 26:28). On that basis only will the deliverance and the blessing be brought in and firmly established.

When Zechariah wrote these things, Greece, mentioned in verse 13, was hardly a power to be reckoned with, though not long after, under Alexander the Great, it was destined to overthrow the Persian power. We may see therefore in the closing verses of this chapter predictions which had a partial fulfilment not long after the prophecy was given, though in their fulness they look on to the end of the age.

CHAPTER TEN

The same thing may be said of the predictions that fill chapter 10, though it opens with solemn words concerning the evils that still were practised among the people. The 'rain' of blessing would descend from God, and not proceed from the 'idols', or 'teraphim', little images by which men sought to probe into future events. All that came from this source was but vanity, and the 'shepherds' of the people, who dealt with such things would have the anger of God against them, for God was going to take up the house of Judah and use them in the execution of judgment in some directions. The word, 'oppressor', in verse 4 has apparently the meaning of, 'ruler'; but, even so, the details of that verse do not refer exactly to the Messiah, but rather to what God will raise up among His people in the last days. It would agree with what we read in Jeremiah 51:20, concerning Israel, 'Thou art My battle axe and weapons of war: for with thee will I break in pieces the nations'. At the end of the age the Lord Himself will execute judgment upon certain nations: upon others He will do so by means of a restored Israel.

Of this our chapter speaks, from verse 5 to the end. It will be an Israel spiritually recreated, and also physically regathered, for God will 'hiss' for them, or, 'pipe' as shepherds used to do in the gathering of their sheep. He will gather them out of Egypt to the south and out of Assyria to the north, as once He smote the river in the days of Moses. Having regathered them, He will strengthen them, so that they 'walk up and down', in His name, which means they will be rightly representing Him on the earth at last. All this clearly looks on to the end of the age.

CHAPTER ELEVEN

The prophetic strain now ceases, and we have to come back in chapter 11 to the actual condition of things among the people to whom Zechariah spoke. The solemn words of governmental judgments here uttered might seem to us strange, had we not the books of Ezra and Nehemiah, which show us the sad departure into flagrant law-breaking which marked the masses of the people, whilst outwardly temple and city were being rebuilt. The prophet foresaw the times of trouble that would come upon the people, when they would still be under the heel of various Gentile powers, and the really godly are designated as the margin of verse 7 reads, 'the flock of slaughter, verily the poor of the flock'.

Commencing with this seventh verse we find the prophet himself beginning to act in a symbolic way as well as speak God's message. He took the two staves, called respectively, 'Beauty' and 'Bands'. Though the poor of the flock were to be fed, the others were to be left, and the shepherds who might have fed them were cut off. We may not be able to say to whom the 'three shepherds' referred, yet the drift of this judgment is plain. While the poor of the flock should be fed, the ungodly majority lost the worldly leaders who might have fed them.

It would appear that in this remarkable incident of the two staves the prophet is led to impersonate the Messiah Himself. His first action was to break the staff called 'Beauty', as a sign that God's covenant 'with all the people', was broken. The word here is in the plural, 'peoples', and we may turn back to Genesis 49:10, where the word had previously occurred in the plural— 'until Shiloh come; and unto Him shall the gathering of the peoples be'. The staff 'Beauty' was broken as a sign that there would be no fulfilment to the unbelieving generation, for when Messiah came in lowliness and not in outward splendour, they would see 'no beauty that we should desire Him' (Isaiah 53:2).

This was followed by the remarkable actions recorded in verses 12 and 13, which prophetically set forth the terrible actions of Judas Iscariot. Matthew 27:3-8, records how accurately this prediction was fulfilled. Messiah, who was the embodiment of all *beauty* was priced at thirty pieces of silver. Judas who fixed the price and got the silver, before committing suicide in his remorse, cast the money down in the temple, thus fulfilling the words, 'in the house of the Lord'; while the chief priests took the silver and used it to buy the potter's field, thus fulfilling the words, 'I ... cast them to the potter'.

The breaking of the second staff followed. If beauty be broken by the rejection of the Messiah, the bands that linked together Judah and Israel were necessarily broken. Christ is the Centre of unity for God's earthly people, just as He is the Centre of unity for the church today. We may therefore see a word of warning and instruction for ourselves in what we have before us. Christendom is much occupied today in efforts to achieve unity, realizing what great power might be wielded by a unified church. Do they recognize that Christ in His beauty must be the Centre of all their thoughts and efforts? If His beauty be broken in their thoughts and efforts, everything in the way of bands will be broken as well.

Having first acted as impersonating the true Shepherd of Israel, the prophet is now bidden so to act as to impersonate the false one, who is to come, as a direct result of the government of God in retribution upon the people. What were the 'instruments' of a foolish shepherd we are not told, but what will mark the false one we are plainly told in verse 16. First, there are four things that he will not do. We quote from Darby's New Translation,

> He 'shall not visit those that are about to perish:' and again, 'neither shall seek that which is strayed away:' and again, 'nor heal that which is wounded:' and once more, 'nor feed that which is sound'.

Readers and writer alike will at once be saying, Why, these four things which the false shepherd does *not* do, are exactly those which the true shepherd *does*, in abundant and perfect measure. False shepherds there were before the true One came, as He indicated in John 10:10, 12, but Zechariah is predicting the coming of that antichrist, of whom the Lord spoke when He said, 'if another shall come in his own name, him ye will receive' (John 5:43). This 'idol', or 'worthless' shepherd will be raised up of God in judgment upon the people, 'in the land', as verse 16 says: that is, he will not be some worldly king in the Gentile world, but the false messiah in Palestine—the second 'beast' of Revelation 13, rather than the first.

Here then is a striking exhibition of the governmental ways of God. The unconverted Jew would not have the true Shepherd, when He came in grace: then they shall have the false, who shall feed himself on their 'fat', and tear them unmercifully, though ultimately he will be destroyed in judgment as verse 17 declares. For the ungodly in Israel the final raising up of the 'idol shepherd', will mean the terrors of the great tribulation.

CHAPTER TWELVE

Having thus plainly predicted the rejection of the true Messiah and Shepherd, and the consequent raising up, in God's governmental wrath, of the antichrist—the worthless shepherd—the following series of predictions concerning the Jews and Jerusalem, are presented as a 'burden' in the first verse of chapter 12. And indeed a burden must rest upon the spirit of the reader as we begin that chapter. The way Jehovah presents Himself is very remarkable. The heavens, the earth, and man himself, have all been formed by Him: and in particular, 'the *spirit* of man', for that is the highest part of man's composite being—the part where man's sinful rebellion against God is most sadly manifested. In the end of the prophecy we shall find man's spirit subjugated and restored.

Here however Judah and Jerusalem are in question, and we learn how they will come into prominence and all the nations of the earth be involved in the controversy; for the word 'people', occurring three times in verses 2 and 3, is really in the plural—the peoples or nations. As we write, the earth is full of disputes, yet there is no darker spot of contention than the little land of Palestine. Many worldly observers fear it may yet become 'the cockpit of the nations'. That it will become just that, is plainly declared in these two verses.

When that hour arrives, God's dealings with Jerusalem will reach their climax, as the opening of chapter 14 declares; but here the point is that the nations will come under judgment. When they besiege it, they will find it a cup of 'trembling', or 'bewilderment', for nothing will proceed as they vainly imagine. It will also be a 'burdensome' stone, far beyond their power to lift or to carry. At last God will be acting for and with His people, and so the whole situation will be transformed. Verse 3 begins, 'And in that day ...'. Another 'day' is going to dawn, and the phrase, 'in that day', occurs again in verses 4, 6, 8, 9 and 11. It is the 'day of the Lord', of which other prophets have spoken.

In that day God will act in judgment upon the nations, but will open His eyes upon Judah, just as Jesus turned and opened His eyes upon Peter, after his sad denial, which started the work of repentance in his heart. Later in our chapter we shall find a very deep work of repentance produced in Israel. But for the moment what the prophet brings before us is the fact that in spite of all the failure and faithlessness that had been marking the people, God would at the end make good His word in their deliverance and blessing. This is ever His way, as we may realize with thankfulness. All the evils that have marked the professing church, and the failures that have marked us, who are true saints of the Lord, will not hinder Him, in making good His purpose.

So, as verses 5-8 declare, God will do a remarkable work in Judah, making them like a fire in the midst of the nations, and giving them precedence over the inhabitants of Jerusalem. The reason for this may be that the people of Jerusalem were always inclined to pride themselves on their privileges, with the temple in their midst, as we see in such Scriptures as Jeremiah 7:4, and Micah 3:11. All false pride will have to be brought low in that solemn hour. Yet God will look upon them in power and blessing, as verse 8 declares. In that day truly, 'the house of David' will be 'as God'; for He who came 'of the seed of David', by His incarnation, is none other than the Son of God, as Romans 1:3 so plainly states, and He will be manifested in glory.

As a result of this the nations that come against Jerusalem in that day will be destroyed, and His glorious manifestation will produce the great work of profound repentance that is foretold in the closing verses of the chapter. It will come to pass when, 'they shall look upon Me whom they have pierced', and have their eyes opened to discover who He is. This explains how it will come to pass that as Psalm 110 says, 'Thy people shall be willing in the day of Thy *power*'. They were unwilling and rejected Him in the day of His *poverty*, of which the closing verses of Psalm 109 speak; nor have they been willing in the day of His *patience*, with which Psalm 110 opens. In the day of His power they will see in glory the One whom they pierced, with tremendous result in their consciences and hearts.

Repentance, as ever, is an intensely individual matter. 'The spirit of grace' will move them, and all thought of deserving anything as under law will be abandoned. A century or so before they had mourned deeply in the 'valley of Megiddon' over the untimely death of Josiah, but now there will be a mourning extending over the whole land, and of such depth that everyone has to be in solitude before their God. Of old, Nathan had to come to David and convict him of grievous sin, saying, 'Thou art the man!'; but now the house of Nathan has to be apart in their own sorrowful self-judgment. Simeon and Levi once were brethren, acting together in an act of cruelty, as Genesis 49:5 indicates, but now their families will be apart, bowed in self-judgment before their God.

Repentance always precedes blessing. It is so as the Gospel is preached today. This fact, we fear, has hardly had its due weight with many of us today. Our commission is that, 'repentance and remission of sins should be preached in His name among all nations'

(Luke 24:47). Have we too lightly skipped over the 'repentance' in our desire to arrive at the 'remission of sins'? By all means say frequently, 'Believe on the Lord Jesus Christ, and thou shalt be saved'. But always remember that was the brief word that Paul gave to a *repentant* man, and not to a careless sinner.

So is it here, as we start chapter 13.

CHAPTER THIRTEEN

When deep repentance thus takes place, a fountain is opened to cleanse from sin and uncleanness. We all know Cowper's hymn, based on this verse, notwithstanding we believe the reference here is not to the blood of Christ, shed long ago, which cleanses from sin judicially; that is, as before the throne of God in judgment, but to that 'clean water', that God will 'sprinkle' upon them, as predicted in Ezekiel 36:25. It was to this verse that our Lord referred, as we believe, when He spoke to Nicodemus of that new birth, which is needful if any are to enter the kingdom of God. It was overlooked by the Jews, so Nicodemus was astonished, at the words of the Lord. As a teacher in Israel, he should have known it, as John 3:10 indicates; for both 'water' and 'the Spirit' of which man needs to be 'born', are mentioned in Ezekiel 36.

At last then there will be a born-again Israel, and as a result of that they will possess a new nature: the unclean spirit will be gone, and the idols and other evil things that once ensnared them will be put away. No more will false prophets appear to deceive. If any should attempt it, their very parents would condemn them to death. Their unreality will be made perfectly manifest, as verse 4 indicates.

Verse 5 begins, 'But he shall say ...'. Who is this 'he'? Verses 5 and 6 present a difficult problem. Some take them as referring to one of the false prophets, just alluded to: others as reverting to the true Shepherd, referred to in the previous chapter, and again very clearly in verse 7; and with this we are inclined to agree. The true Shepherd took the place of the 'Hebrew Servant', as indicated in the opening verses of Exodus 21, and was pierced amongst those to whom He came in the spirit of friendship. He took the humble place, and one of suffering, even among men. And there was far deeper suffering beyond this.

Verse 7 predicts that far greater matter. Israel nationally were God's sheep, and their sins and apostasy had a twofold effect. It stirred up God's governmental retribution in this world, of which the prophet had much to say; and it also raised the far more serious matter of God's eternal judgment in the life to come. The true Shepherd was to meet that in such fashion that Jehovah's sword was to awake against Him. The sword that had been awakened by the persistent sins of the faithless sheep, was to smite not them but the holy Shepherd.

'The Man that is My Fellow'—these words may have been an enigma to the prophet who wrote them, for 1 Peter 1:10-11, tells us that often the Old Testament prophets had to discover they were saying things, the full meaning of which would only appear in an age to come: the privileged age in which we live. These words are no enigma to us, who can read Romans 1:3, and learn that He who became 'seed of David according to the flesh' was none other than 'His Son Jesus Christ'. When the Son of God assumed Manhood in holiness and perfection, there was indeed a Man that could be called Jehovah's Fellow. He could take the place of sinful men and allow the judgment sword to awake against Himself.

But the immediate effect of the smiting of the Shepherd would be the scattering of the sheep, on the one hand, but also the turning of God's hand upon the little ones. The children of Israel had been scattered 'because there is no shepherd', as Ezekiel 34:5 says; but since the smiting of the true Shepherd, a far more serious and prolonged scattering has taken place, and yet the 'little ones' have not been forgotten but rather remembered for blessing.

If we turn to Isaiah 1:25, we find the same expression, 'I will turn My hand', and the context there indicates that the turning of His hand means blessing, when for His adversaries there is judgment. If we read the closing chapters of the Gospels and the opening chapters of the Acts, we see God turning His hand in blessing upon the 'little ones', when the great ones among the Jews were pursuing their way in blindness to the hour of their great scattering. The great verse we have been considering has indeed been wondrously fulfilled.

And the two verses that conclude the chapter will be fulfilled with equal exactness in their season, for they refer, we judge, to what God will bring to pass at the end of this age, when He will deal with a people to be found in the land at that time. In Ezekiel 20:34-38, we learn how God will deal with the people scattered throughout the nations, purging them before He brings them into the land for blessing. Here we learn what He will do to such as may be left 'in all the land', in the last days. Judgment will fall on two-thirds of them, and only a third will come through into blessing. And those blessed will have to pass through the fire of tribulation, which will refine them in a spiritual sense, and bring them at last into vital connection with God. They will truly own Him, and He will own them in blessing.

We must keep this in our minds as we begin to read chapter 14.

CHAPTER FOURTEEN

When the day of the Lord arrives, there will come the moment of supreme crisis for Jerusalem. God will allow the most determined adversaries to have their way for a brief time. It has ever been thus. When God begins to work, the adversary is stirred to put forth his power to the utmost but only to find his efforts over-ruled for ultimate good. Thus it was on that occasion that stands out above all else, as is recorded in Acts 4:26-28. The actions of the adversary only help to accomplish what God had determined from the outset. How great a comfort is this fact for us today.

The final siege of Jerusalem, that verse 2 indicates, we believe to be that which is predicted in the latter part of Daniel 11, as the act of 'the king of the north'. In that chapter, verses 36-39, we have at the time of the end, the king, who will do according to his own will, exalting himself, and magnifying himself above every god, and not regarding 'the God of his fathers', whom we regard as being identical with the 'idol shepherd', and with the second 'beast' of Revelation 13. Against this king, as Daniel reveals, will be found both 'the king of the south' and 'the king of the north', and it is the latter who will 'go forth with great fury to destroy, and utterly to make away many'; and who will finally plant his palace, 'in the glorious holy mountain'. And Daniel's terse summary of the result is, 'yet he shall come to his end, and none shall help him'.

The two 'beasts' of Revelation are not antagonistic, but acting in concert. The attack of Gog, of the land of Magog, predicted in Ezekiel 38 and 39, is against the land of Palestine generally, and not specially Jerusalem, when the land has been brought back from the sword; so these great actors of the last days cannot well be identified with what we have before us here. This leaves the king of the north, who is called the Assyrian in Isaiah's prophecy, as the one whose attack will fulfil verse 2 of our chapter, though all nations will be involved in the tremendous happenings of those days. It will be, as Zechariah 12 has told us, 'a burdensome stone for all nations'.

No city, we are told, has been besieged so many times as Jerusalem, and here we learn that this one, the last, will be up to a point a complete success; and then, just before all is complete, the attacker will come to his end and none shall help him. How this will come to pass verse 3 reveals. Jehovah will suddenly and unexpectedly intervene in power. When He fought against Egypt at the exodus, He swept the whole Egyptian army into death— 'there remained not so much as one of them'. In Hezekiah's day He intervened against Assyria, and 185,000 dead lay upon the earth. What He did of old, He will do again.

But verses 4 and 5 furnish us with further details of a very remarkable character. When He thus appears, He will have 'feet', which 'shall stand in that day upon the mount of Olives', and He will have 'all the saints' with Him. In the light of the New Testament we recognize with joy that the 'LORD', the 'LORD my God' of our

Scripture is none other than our blessed Lord Jesus Christ. His feet left the mount of Olives, when as the earth-rejected One, He ascended to the glory of heaven. On that same spot His feet shall stand, when He returns in power and great glory in judgment upon His foes.

When He does thus come, a great convulsion will break the surface of the earth. We have not heard of Palestine as a land much subject to earthquakes, during recent centuries. There was one in the days of Uzziah, to which our passage refers, and there was another at the moment Jesus died, as recorded in Matthew 27:51. From that time onward has there been another in Jerusalem? —we wonder. At any rate, there is going to be another, as predicted here. An earthquake, when He died the death of the cross, in extremest humiliation! An earthquake, when He returns in splendour and majesty! How wonderfully suitable are the ways of our God!

It is quite clear, we think, that the overthrow of the two beasts of Revelation 13 at Armageddon is something distinct from that which we have before us, though we do not know of any Scripture which makes plain which of the two overthrows precedes the other.

As the result of the earthquake a way of escape is made for the remnant—the godly remnant, as we suppose—in the moment of their extremity. Saints will be delivered on earth, while the heavenly saints will appear in glory with the triumphant Christ. The translation of verses 6 and 7 is somewhat obscure, but they evidently emphasize the fact that again, just as it was on the day of the crucifixion, there will be atmospheric changes in the heavens as well as the earthquake in the surface of the earth. There will be light at eventide, just when naturally we expect darkness to be falling on the scene.

Verses 8 and 10 further show that the earthquake will produce other great changes in Palestine, both in the flowing forth of waters and in the formation of a plain with Jerusalem lifted up in the midst of it. This agrees with the predictions in the later chapters of Ezekiel. All will be preparatory for the Jerusalem and temple that is to arise in millennial splendour, when, as verse 9 says, the Lord will be King over the whole earth. Subsidiary kings there may be, as Isaiah 52:15 seems to indicate; but He is indeed the King of kings. At last the great era of peace will have arrived.

But it will not come to pass without judgment of a very severe kind falling upon the sinful nations, as verses 12-15 show. The terrible effects of judgment on the bodies of men are given in verse 12, and these have, in our day, been likened to the effects produced on the survivors after the fall and explosion of an atom bomb. But in addition to this there will be the internecine destruction of which verse 13 speaks. And further Judah will enter into the conflict, and much wealth will be laid up for the coming day.

We must remember that, though the king of the north may be specially concerned in this attack on Jerusalem, all the nations will be involved as stated in verse 2, and so these tremendous warlike judgments will be widely felt in all directions, and hence we get in verse 16 the expression, 'every one that is left'. We believe that this expression signifies that only a very small proportion of mankind will be left. At the present time many men of foresight are concerned about the very rapid rise in the population of the earth, particularly in nations like China, India and Japan. The over-population that they anticipate half a century ahead may never come to pass if the day of the Lord arrives before that, for there is not only to take place the warrior-judgment here indicated, but also the sessional-judgment of Matthew 25, when the 'goats' are separated from the 'sheep', and go down to destruction.

Those that are left will year by year come up to Jerusalem to worship and to keep the feast of tabernacles. When that feast was instituted under the law it was typical of the rest of the millennial age, which will then have been established. So it will be observed as a memorial of the fact that what had been typified had now been actually established, and not to observe it would result in punishment.

The two verses that close this prophecy emphasize the holiness that becomes everybody and everything that is brought into contact with God. Holiness, we have been told, becomes His house for ever. In the coming age it will be stamped upon the most ordinary and the most humble things, such as bells that jingle round the necks of horses and little bowls that have some part to play in the temple services. It is worthwhile noticing that horses are mentioned here, for we might be inclined to ask, But, will not these marvellous inventions in the matter of transport be further increased and expanded in that day? The answer must be that there is no mention of these inventions in Scripture, but the reverse. In that day, instead of men flying all over the earth in their unsatisfied desires, the picture is rather of a man sitting restfully in contentment under his own vine and fig-tree. The knowledge of God will then be filling the earth, and it is this that really satisfies the heart. God in His holiness will, so to speak, have come in; and consequently from the house of the Lord, the Canaanite will have been permanently cast out.

These closing words of our prophet might strike us as rather unusual, did we not remember that the continual trouble that menaced the returned remnant of Israel amongst whom Zechariah prophesied was this very matter of marrying Canaanite wives, and even giving some of the Canaanites, related to them by these marriages, a place in the chambers of the rebuilt temple. This thing which had been so great a snare to them, would be gone for ever.

And as we close our meditations on this prophet, let us not forget that a similar tendency has ever been a great snare amongst Christians. What was it that underlay all the disorders that marred the church at Corinth? It comes clearly to light in Paul's second letter to them, when in chapter 6 he felt his 'mouth' was 'open unto you', as he put it. He put his finger upon the real trouble; and it was their 'unequal' yoking with unbelievers. All through the church's history this has been one main source of trouble and dishonour. It is so today, we have sadly to confess.

May God give us all grace and strength to flee from it!

Malachi

CHAPTER ONE

Unlike the prophets Haggai and Zechariah, who furnish us with dates in regard to their utterances, Malachi gives us no such details. It seems certain, however, that he wrote about a century later; hence his words reveal how little effect the ministry of these two earlier prophets had produced amongst the masses of the people in the land. As we read through the short book we shall notice that every statement the prophet has to make—usually by way of correction—is repudiated. The people and their leaders were not prepared to admit anything. They were quite self-satisfied.

Satisfied with themselves, they were dissatisfied with God. Hence when the prophet made his first assertion— 'I have loved you, saith the Lord'—they challenge it at once. Many troubles afflicted the Palestinian Jews in those years, which God permitted as a chastisement, because of their state: these afflictions they resented, regarding them as harshness and contrary to love. Hence they challenged the assertion, in an insolent way, asking, 'Wherein hast Thou loved us?'

The answer of God to this was to recall them to what marked His attitude and action from the beginning. He had loved Jacob and hated Esau. Human opinion would have reversed this: Jacob stooped to crooked and crafty schemes: Esau a fine manly fellow. Yes, but the 'birth-right', which carried with it, we believe, the advent of the Messiah, meant so little to Esau, that he sold it for a bowl of pottage, whereas Jacob esteemed it of highest worth. Here we have perhaps the earliest forecast that 'What think ye of Christ' is the test.

Now God maintained His attitude of judgment against Esau, as verses 4 and 5 show, and thus magnified Himself '*beyond* the border of Israel' (New Trans.). But, on the contrary, Israel had been brought into relationship with God, who in regard to them had taken a father's place, as verse 6 shows. Love had established this relationship. How had they acted as to it?

To them God was both Father and Master. Both honour and fear should have been His, and yet the very priests had despised His name. They should have been the very first to have revered His name, and have acted consistently with it. They had not done so, and this brought the hand of God in government against them. They treated this as a denial of His original love towards their nation.

But it was not so. Nor are the fatherly chastisements that come upon His saints today, any denial of His love, as Hebrews 12:6 plainly declares. Let us remember this, and never ask, when trying circumstances arise—If God loves me, why does He send, or permit this?

In Malachi's day the priests did not for one moment admit the charge laid against them. They repudiated it saying, 'Wherein have we despised Thy name?' This brought forth a more specific accusation as to their offering 'polluted bread' upon God's altar; and verse 8 gives further details as to this. The kind of offerings they were bringing meant that they treated 'the table of the Lord' as 'contemptible'. It was not, we judge, that they were saying this in so many words, but that was what their actions declared; for, as we know, actions speak louder than words, and God knows perfectly how to interpret them.

The fact was that they were offering to God animals that they would never present to a secular governor; and further, as verse 10 shows, they expected to make some material gain for the simplest things they did in the temple service. They were putting their own things first and treating God's service as subservient to themselves. Has this no voice for us? We believe it has very definitely. The flesh in each of us would naturally and easily put our own earthly interests first, and treat 'the kingdom of God and His righteousness' as something that may conveniently fill up any little gaps left as we pursue our own things. It is all too easy to forget the Lord's words in Matthew 6:32.

Through the prophet God made it plain that though they profaned His name, He would yet make it 'great' as we see in verse 11, and that even among the heathen, whom they so greatly despised. When the wise and mighty utterly fail, God takes up the weak and despised to achieve His ends, as is stated so clearly in 1 Corinthians 1:26-29. And what about the fulfilment of this prediction? It will be literally fulfilled in the coming millennial age, but we can make a spiritual application even today. We have humbly to admit that many of us, easy-going, English-speaking Christians, living amid luxuries, may have to take a back seat in the coming

Kingdom of reward, compared with simple saints—often but babes in Christ—who live and die for their faith under Communist or Romish persecution.

The three verses that close this chapter again bring home the evils that were prevalent. Twice further the prophet's charges home upon what they were saying—'The table of the Lord is polluted', and also, as to the service rendered, 'What a weariness is it!' They themselves had polluted it, and if the heart be not in God's service, what a weariness it can become! To have 'a form of godliness' without the 'power', leads to all the evils delineated in 2 Timothy 3:1-5. We must never forget the closing words of the chapter. In Christ God is known to us as the God of all grace, but at the same time He is 'a great King', and His name is 'dreadful', or 'to be revered', among the nations. His grace does not cancel out His majesty; indeed His majesty enhances His grace.

CHAPTER TWO

Chapter 2 continues the solemn warnings that have been occupying us. The priests, who were, so to speak, the finest specimens of the tribe of Levi, are further denounced for their sinful practices, and warned that already a curse lay upon them. They are reminded in verses 4-6, of God's original covenant with that tribe, when for a time they answered to it and walked suitably before their God. Now all was sadly changed. As ever, God viewed their defection in the light of the original calling and behaviour. How do we stand? we may well ask, in the light of the original calling and behaviour of the church, as we see it in the opening chapters of the Acts. Another matter to search our hearts very deeply.

Another very serious thing about the priests of those days comes to light in verses 7 and 8. The priest was intended to be a 'messenger', who should possess a knowledge of the law, and so be able to convey it to the masses of the people. Though the 'law of truth' was in the mouth of Levi at the outset, it was not so in Malachi's day. It was departed from the hearts and lips of the priests. They were not only out of the way themselves, but they were a cause of stumbling, leading many others out of the way. Thus they had corrupted God's original covenant with their tribe.

Once again we have to note how God always reverts to that which He establishes at the beginning. Man's beginnings are imperfect. His inventions are crude at the outset, and improved as time goes on. God establishes that which is perfect in its time and place. If men think to improve, they actually only deface. In the things of God today, let us remember this. As soon as departure from the faith of Christ became manifest, the Spirit of God began to emphasize 'that which was from the beginning', as John's epistles show. Amid the confusions of Christendom we are on safe and right ground if we revert to the simplicity, both in faith and in practice, of that which was divinely established at the outset of the dispensation.

Verses 9-13 that follow, show how departure from God's purpose and plan had disorganized and corrupted all behaviour amongst the people themselves. The priests had become contemptible in the popular view, and false dealing abounded amongst the people. Idolatry crept in, and the holiness of the Lord outraged. When this brought down God's judgment upon them, there was much outcry and covering the altar with tears, but this was not real repentance, but only a protest against their troubles. Hence God paid no regard to it.

This disregard on God's part was an offence to them, and they in petulant fashion asked, 'Wherefore?' This led to a more specific charge being laid against them. There was much marital infidelity: much putting away of their wives in treacherous fashion, in disregard of God's original purpose in making both man and his wife to be one. Here once more we see that God's original design stands unshaken, no matter how far it may be forsaken and forgotten. We also see that when God is ignored and His things forgotten, confusion soon ensues as to our own things.

We have to notice also that when evil of this sort is allowed, it not only spreads but persists. When some centuries later our Lord was on earth, the Pharisees came with the question, 'Is it lawful for a man to put away his wife for every cause?' (Matthew 19:3), which infers that these loose practices were still common. We know how our Lord referred them at once to what God established at the beginning.

Having read thus far, the last verse of Malachi 2 does not surprise us. They had indeed wearied the Lord with their words, refusing to admit any charge that had to be brought against them, but rather challenging the accusation in very insolent fashion. But even this remonstrance they met in the same self-satisfied way, asking, 'Wherein have we wearied Him?' They were not prepared to admit anything. They would rather cast an aspersion on God Himself.

So the prophet is led to bring home the charge against them in two specific ways. First, there were those who sought to make God to be, so to speak, a partner in their evil, as though He approved of it, treating as good that which was evil. This is a religious trick, not uncommon, we fear, in our day. All too many would claim they are serving God and pleasing Him in practising things wholly astray from His truth. The priests and people, that Malachi addressed, were religious folk, and this is an evil specially seen in the religious sphere.

But then again, there were others, who did not attempt to make God a partner in their evil. They were less crafty, but more bold. They apparently challenged God's judgment, when He by the prophet challenged them. Their question, 'Where is the God of judgment?' may not have insinuated that He had no right to judge, but rather that He had not exercised His right of judgment in the matters that were in question. Whatever was their exact meaning, they evidently endeavoured to thrust God, and His word, out of the whole matter. The spirit, that lay behind this form of reasoning in self-defence, is not dead in our day.

CHAPTER THREE

The full answer to all this appears as we commence to read chapter 3. God Himself was going to intervene in a very personal way. In the first verse we have in the first place, 'My messenger', or 'angel'. 'He is to prepare the way before Me'; the 'Me' here evidently being Jehovah. Then, thirdly, there is the 'Lord', or 'Master', who is the 'Messenger', or, 'Angel of the covenant'; clearly distinguished from the angel first mentioned. In this very close way the coming Messiah is identified with the Jehovah who sends Him. In this remarkable verse the two advents are predicted, though not clearly distinguished: a feature we also see in Isaiah 61:2. At His first advent the messenger sent in advance was clearly

John the Baptist, who prepared the way of the Lord, and came in the spirit and power of Elijah, though not the Elijah of which Malachi 4:5 speaks, for he is to come before the great and dreadful day of the Lord in judgment. John came after the fashion of Elijah, but before the coming of the Messiah in grace, who is the Master, identified here with Jehovah.

Suddenly to His temple the 'Lord', the 'Master' came. And He was the One in whom they delighted, as a matter of theory, in expectation, though, when He did appear, they saw no beauty in Him, that they should desire Him, as Isaiah had predicted. Hence He was rejected and crucified as we know; though that is not predicted here. In contrast thereto our thoughts are turned at once to His second advent, when He will be like fire and soap in their testing and cleansing power, and who will then be able to stand before Him? He will then be in majesty on the throne, and not standing as the Prisoner in Pilate's judgment hall.

So, as we said, both advents are here predicted; and the exact fulfilment of the first part gives us the assurance that the second part will in its season be fulfilled with equal exactitude.

In Malachi's day this was not apparent, and the point to the people of his time was that things would be brought to an issue, and their state judged by an intervention of God, such as they had never before known. All their hypocritical self-satisfaction would collapse, and reality be brought to light when He appeared.

It may be profitable now to digress a little and point out two things. First, let us observe that behind all this state of things so clearly manifested, lay the work of the adversary, making it certain that when Christ came in grace, He would be rejected. A few centuries passed and the state of things exposed by Malachi, developed into the Phariseeism and Sadduceeism, exposed in the Gospels and in the Acts. The former ardently followed a religion of outward observances; the latter favoured something of a more intellectual type, and therefore were unbelieving as to certain things that did not appeal to their reason. Both therefore were absolutely self-confident as to their own position, and bitterly resented anything that undermined it. The spirit that we see among priests and people in Malachi's day was so intensified, that when the Messiah did arrive His coming was no joy to them. This we see in Matthew 2:3. That an evil king like Herod should be troubled, when tidings of His birth came by the wise men from the east, need not surprise us. But look at the words, 'and all Jerusalem with him'. Let us each underline in our minds that word, 'all'. It evidently signifies—Pharisees and Sadducees included. True, these religious men had a knowledge of their Scriptures, for they could at once quote Micah 5:2, in reply to Herod's demand. Yet the only practical use made of their knowledge was to furnish Herod with an opportunity to kill the infant Messiah. There is no record of their doing anything about it, or welcoming Him.

There was of course a work of God, going on amongst the people in Malachi's day, as we shall presently see, and this worked out also, and was maintained till the coming of Christ as we see in the lovely picture of devout souls, who gladly received Him, given us in the opening of Luke's gospel. Through the years, however, these were few in number and comparatively unknown.

There is a second thing we ask our readers to observe. This strain of self-satisfied complacency, that resents and repudiates all criticism, evident in Malachi's day, and more decisively manifested when Christ came, is predicted in Revelation 3, as characterizing the end of the church's history. We refer to the Laodicean church, that felt itself to be so 'rich, and increased with goods', doubtless of a spiritual sort, as well as a material, that they had 'need of nothing'. To have need of nothing is for all practical purposes to lay claim to perfection, and therefore to be beyond all criticism; and bitterly to resent it, if offered, even as they had begun to do when Malachi prophesied.

And let us note another feature. The outward ruin of Israel fairly started when 'that woman Jezebel' was married to Ahab, and nearly diverted the ten tribes to the worship of Baal. Then with the two tribes there was that time of deadness Godward in the days of Jeremiah, ended by the captivity. And then the mercy of God, permitting a remnant to return to the land and re-establish the temple worship; and amongst these were a number of really godly and devout souls. It was amongst that remnant that the evils, we have had before us, had developed.

Now notice a painful analogy. It may not be very pronounced and distinct, but it is there nevertheless. The addresses to the seven churches give us a prophetic outline of 'things which must shortly come to pass', as Revelation 1:1 states; and when we reach the latter part of chapter 2, we find 'that woman Jezebel', dominating things in the Thyatira stage. And this is followed by the spiritual death that marked Sardis, and then some measure of recovery in Philadelphia, not anything great, for their strength was 'little', and they had the rather negative virtues of keeping the word of the Lord, when others were forsaking it, and of not denying His name, when others were doing so.

But then comes Laodicea. If God has granted a measure of recovery during the last century or two, and some of us have entered into a heritage of spiritual blessing, let us beware of this Laodicean spirit of self-occupation and self-conceit which so naturally would entangle us. Today we have not only the high-class intellectualist, who believes he has a modernistic version of Christianity, which is beyond all criticism, but also a mystical type, great on the experimental side of things, who feel they have entered into something which is also beyond all criticism. They feel 'rich' because they increase in 'goods', in the form of increased light and further revelations.

We see the Laodicean delusion, if we may so call it, beginning in the days of Malachi. It is sadly evident in our day, and hence we need to be warned against it, for it is a deep-seated tendency of the flesh, which is in every one of us. The more worldly-minded believer may be tempted to glory in wisdom or nobility, and the more spiritually-minded to glory in spiritual experiences, imagined or real, but the only safe ground of boasting is that stated by the Apostle Paul, 'He that glorieth, let him glory in the Lord' (1 Corinthians 1:31).

The first verse of our chapter, as we saw, has in it predictions that found a fulfilment at the first advent of Christ. The second and third verses, however, make it clear that the main emphasis is on His second coming. Then it is that the fire of the refiner will come into action with purifying effect, and this means judgment as verse 5 states. The bringing of the advents together is not unusual in Old Testament prophecy. Take the later chapters of Isaiah for instance, where the humbled 'Servant' of Jehovah and the mighty 'Arm' of Jehovah, achieving His purpose, come before us. Chapter 53, which predicts the sufferings of the Servant, begins by asking, 'To whom is the Arm of the Lord revealed?' In other words, 'Who identifies the glorious and irresistible Arm with the despised and humbled Servant?' This was not so plain in the days when the prophets spoke; but very plain in ours; so that we can all reply—Thank God, we do with joy identify them.

What His second advent will accomplish is stated in verses 4 and 5. There will be first a work of purification, and at last the offerings of a restored people will be pure and acceptable, as it had been at the beginning. The 'fuller's soap' will have had its effect. So also the 'refiner's fire' will have come into action judging and removing all the sins and evils, then so prevalent among the people. The fear of God will be established in every heart, and express itself in life.

And the guarantee of all this is found in verse 6. It is the unchangeable character of Jehovah. We might have expected the next words to be, 'Therefore ye sons of Jacob *must be* consumed'; but they are just the opposite. God exercises much forbearance, and He has power to reach His own purpose in the end. The Apostle Paul asks the question, 'Hath God cast away His people?'; and he at once answers, 'God forbid' (Romans 11:1). At the time of the second advent, judgment will fall on the Jew, yet a godly remnant of the 'sons of Jacob' will be preserved and blessed. The same thing of course is true today.

In verse 7 the prophet returns to his earlier theme, and lays against them the general charge of having departed from God and His Word, with the promise, if they returned to Him, He would return to them. The charge was most apparently true, yet they did not admit it, but rather called it in question. Again they resented and repudiated these words. So, in verse 8, the prophet brings against them a specific charge. They robbed God, by withholding that which was His due, according to the law.

Did they admit this? No. Once more they challenged the accusation. They had to be told that 'tithes and offerings' had been withheld, and so what should have been given to God had been spent on themselves. This it was that brought a curse upon them in the government of God. At the opening of Haggai's prophecy we saw how their ancestors were doing the same kind of thing, though perhaps on a smaller scale, when they stopped the building of the house of the Lord, and started the building of nice houses for themselves. In both cases the practice was to give the first place to their own things, and then any surplus to be given to God.

And what is the practice in Christendom today; and even among true Christians? We fear that very similar charge could be maintained against all too many of us. Small wonder then, if we see but small result from the work in which we do engage.

Thus they had been robbing God, and the prophet had to confront them with this solemn fact. But he also was authorized to assure them that if they reversed their practice and gave to God His due, there would open 'the windows of heaven' and pour out more than they could receive. The emphasis here is of course on material things for as the Apostle tells us, God 'is able to do

exceeding abundantly above all that we ask or think'
(Ephesians 3:20). So there is no limit on His side,
though such failure, and so often, on our side.

The delightful state of things promised in verses 11 and
12, will only be reached in the age to come, when Christ
returns, for only then will God be fully acknowledged
and His claims fully met. Palestine will at last be a
'delightsome land', when Christ is on the throne. In
Malachi's day things were different, and the people in
their spirits far from God. This comes before us once
more, and for the last time in verses 13 and 14.

Their words had indeed been 'stout' against the Lord, as
this short book bears abundant witness. Yet they did not
admit even this. If we have counted rightly, the prophet
cites what they were saying no less that twelve times,
and of these twelve no less than eight were cases of
priests and people indignantly repudiating the
accusation that God had to bring against them. They
were not prepared to admit anything, and resented the
words of God. They would not even admit that they had
resented and repudiated the truth.

If we glance at such scriptures as Jeremiah 2:30; 5:3;
7:28; and Zephaniah 3:2; we find that a similar spirit
prevailed among the people in Jerusalem just before its
destruction by Nebuchadnezzar. They who refuse
'correction', thereby claim to be all they should be. In
Malachi's day, as we are seeing, all correction was being
refused; and the same thing meets us in Revelation 3,
since Laodicea is so rich as to have need of nothing, and
therefore no need of correction. So again we have to
remind ourselves of our danger in this direction, which
is specially acute as we draw near to the end of the
church's history.

The disastrous effects of this spirit we see in verses 14 and 15. The people had been serving God in this official and ceremonial way, and they felt they got nothing out of it in the form of material gain, which was what they wanted. Hence their sense of real values was entirely perverted. In their view to be proud was to be 'happy'; and evil amongst them became exalted. This is just what we see in the record of the Gospels; the proud Pharisee was accounted the happy man. Because of this, when on the mountain the Lord 'opened His mouth and taught', the very first of His beatitudes was, 'Blessed are the poor in spirit; for theirs is the kingdom of heaven' (Matthew 5:3). To be 'poor in spirit' is the exact opposite to being proud in spirit, as the leaders were in Malachi's day, as well as in the day when Christ came; and we fear it is not absent in our day also.

In verse 16 we find something more in keeping with our Lord's beatitude. Amidst all this proud self-conceit and intolerance of correction, there was found a godly remnant, who are characterized as 'they that feared the Lord'. This 'fear' produced a reverence for God and His will, that made Him the governing factor in their lives. This at once put them into complete contrast with the mass of priests and people, that surrounded them.

Certain features that marked these pious folk are given, and we find them very instructive. The fear of the Lord was the fundamental thing, but this led them to think 'upon His name'. They recognized that they were a people called into relationship with Jehovah, according to the way He had revealed Himself to their fathers, and they were therefore responsible to live lives in keeping with the revelation made, so that His name might be honoured. Consequently, they could be acknowledged as 'righteous', and as serving God, as verse 18 shows.

These features, we have just noticed, were Godward, but they led to a happy state of things manward; that is, among themselves. They did not remain as a number of isolated units, but recognized each other and sought one another's company for spiritual help and encouragement. This they did 'often', and their intercourse was of so good a character that though it has not been recorded on earth, a heavenly record has been kept. No small honour this!

We turn to the opening chapters of Luke's Gospel, and we find that though several centuries have passed a godly remnant still persists. And here we are permitted to read a few of their utterances. Let us take as a sample what old Anna spoke about when she went visiting 'all them that looked for redemption in Jerusalem'—they could not have been a very great number; could they? — her theme was this, 'she spake of **Him**'. The advent of the long looked-for Messiah was her only theme.

Once again we may turn to Revelation 3, for in the address to the assembly at Philadelphia we find similar good features appearing. Though having only a little strength they too had kept the word of the Lord and had not denied His name—and the name, in the light of which they walked, went in its claims beyond anything known in Malachi's day, or even in the day when Anna spake of Him.

It is an encouragement to know that, however dark the day, God will maintain a witness to Himself. Let us seek grace and humility from God to be within that witness today; for, as this scripture shows, it is of value in His eyes. A day is coming when these obscure, unknown saints of Malachi's day are going to be owned as 'Mine', by the Lord of hosts and that will take place when He will 'make up My jewels'; the inference being that He will count even them, as being jewels in His sight. A person might point to a casket of jewels and tell us they are but small pieces of stone. Yes, we should reply, but they possess the property of reflecting light, and sparkling in various hues as it is turned upon them. The figure therefore is an apt one, for the saints of God are partakers of the divine nature, and so have the capacity to reflect the light into which they are brought. In Revelation 21, the foundations of the heavenly city are precious stones, and in them the names of the twelve apostles of the Lamb.

CHAPTER FOUR

But the day when the Lord of hosts makes up His jewels will be a day of discrimination, and therefore of judgment as well as blessing. This comes clearly to light as we commence to read the last chapter of this short prophecy. The earth is of course in view, and when judgment does arrive it will be final and complete. Neither root nor branch will be left as far as the wicked are concerned. The Sun of righteousness will arise to exterminate the wicked, while He will bring healing and full blessing to those who fear His name.

In the Old Testament the Lord Jesus—the coming One—has been presented under a variety of beautiful figures; this closing figure comes home to us all, we trust, with singular force. He who has read through the 39 books, up to this point, has certainly surveyed a very dark scene with here and there little patches of light. We now close with the promise of God's resplendent day, introduced by the rising of the 'Sun', in whom all true light is concentrated, and who is specially to be the display of, and the enforcer of, righteousness in perfection. In a world ruined by sin everything is *wrong*: hence if an order of things is to be established according to God, the first consideration must be what is *right*. This is seen even in the Gospel that we preach today, as expounded in the epistle of the Romans. Paul was not ashamed of the Gospel since it is the power of God unto salvation; and it is that because in it righteousness of God is proclaimed, and made available by faith for sinners such as we were. Behind the righteousness lies of course the love of God, but that is not actually mentioned in the epistle until we reach chapter 5.

If righteousness be fully established it must mean the elimination of all that is wrong. Hence the beams of that glorious 'Sun' will burn like an oven destroying the ungodly, while bringing healing and fertility to those who fear God.

How different is the final presentation of the Lord Jesus in the New Testament, where He comes before us as the bright, Morning Star, which is the harbinger of the coming day. No thought of judgment enters here for, as the Lord Jesus Himself says, He sent His angel 'to testify unto you these things in the churches'. For only those who are in 'the churches', have the knowledge of Him, who is the 'Morning Star', and who are on the look-out for Him, while the world is still in darkness before the rising of the 'Sun'. When the Morning Star appears, there will be the first sign of the rising of the Sun of righteousness, and the coming of the day of the Lord; for there will be the 'rapture', or snatching away of saints, both dead and living, to present them before the Father in their heavenly home.

We now have to call attention to verse 4 of our chapter. It might strike us at first as a rather extraordinary command to be interjected at this very late hour in Israel's history, about a thousand years after the law was given through Moses. But enshrined in it we see two important principles. First, the law was given for 'all Israel' and it was given 'with the statutes and judgments'. The people in the land, to whom specially Malachi wrote, were comparatively few and in surroundings very different from the days of Moses, or even the days of David and Solomon, but if a man was an Israelite the whole law, in all its details was still binding upon him, and to be obeyed.

And in the second place, not only was it a case of *all the law* for *every* Israelite, wherever he might be, but it was also a case of *all the time*. The fact that many centuries had passed made no difference. In Malachi's day some Israelite might have been saying to himself—But circumstances are so different today; surely a lot of these minor details of the law are not so binding as at the beginning. Here then was the necessary word for one such as that.

Exactly the same tendency confronts us today. As an instance of what we mean, take Paul's first epistle to the Corinthians, written at the outset of our dispensation, nineteen centuries ago. There was much disorder among the Corinthian Christians, so the Apostle was inspired to lay down the order that should prevail amongst them both in their individual lives, and in their functions as members of the body of Christ, which is the church. In chapter 14 he lays down the Divine administration for their assembly meetings, and concludes by calling upon them to recognize that the directions he gives are 'the commandments of the Lord'. Are any of us tempted to say, or even to think, —Yes, but the changes that have supervened during these many centuries are far greater than at any other period of the world's history; surely we are hardly bound to these small details of assembly life and practice. If we are so tempted let us consider this verse.

It is happily true that we, 'are not under the law, but under grace' (Romans 6:14), and yet we are furnished with many commandments. The commandments of the law were given, that by keeping them men might establish their righteousness before God. This they never did. Grace brings salvation to us who believe, and then teaches us to live sober, righteous and godly lives, as is stated in Titus 2:11-12, and then issues commandments, to guide us in so doing. But *commandments* they are, and not to be brushed aside while the dispensation lasts.

What we have indicated is further supported by the closing chapter of the New Testament. We have already noticed how Revelation 22 ends with the 'Morning Star', rather than the 'Sun of righteousness', and now we notice that it closes also with a strong assertion of the sacred integrity of the Word of God. No man is to add to, or take away from, its words. This has doubtless special reference to the Revelation, but coming at the close of the New Testament, we believe it has reference to the whole New Testament revelation, in a secondary way, just as the verse we have been considering applies to the whole Old Testament revelation.

In these closing words the minds of the people were not only carried back to Moses, but also onward to Elijah, as we see in verse 5. Through Moses the law had been given. By Elijah the ten tribes had been recalled to God and His law, in days when they were almost swamped by the worship of Baal. Before the coming of the predicted day of the Lord an 'Elijah' is to appear. We may remember that when John the Baptist was asked if he were Elijah, he answered, No. Yet he came in the spirit and power of Elijah, so that in regard to the first coming our Lord could say, 'If ye will receive it, this is Elias, which was for to come' (Matthew 11:14).

But the first coming of our Lord was the introduction of the day of grace. It is His second coming in power and glory that will introduce 'the great and dreadful day of the Lord'. Hence, we judge, this prediction in its fulness must still await its fulfilment. In Revelation 11:3-6, we read of 'two witnesses', marked by features in their testimony, reminiscent of Moses and Elijah, and these precede the second coming of the Lord. We may connect the Elijah of our verse with one of these. What we can say with assurance is that God ever raises up adequate witness, and gives adequate warning, before He acts in judgment.

What is stated in the last verse may seem rather obscure, but if we read Luke 1:17, the bearing of it is plain. The 'disobedient' will be turned to 'the wisdom of the just', and thus a people prepared for the Lord. Thus a godly remnant will be found, otherwise the whole earth would be smitten with a curse.

The Old Testament is the history of man under the law: hence its last word is, 'curse'. The New Testament is the story of the appearing of God's grace: hence the last word is, 'The grace of the Lord Jesus Christ be with all the saints' (New Trans.). How happy are we to live in a day when grace is on the throne, reigning through righteousness!

Appendix:
The Lost Diadem[2]

To say that an outstanding feature of the present time is the almost universal spirit of unrest is to utter merely a platitude. The thing is so obtrusive as to be patent even to a frivolous mind.

Clashing of interests, conflict, upheaval and unrest are no new things in the earth. When, since the entrance of sin, did they not exist? Admitting this, however, we venture to affirm that the present epidemic of unrest and upheaval has assumed such proportions that it may justly be termed the leading feature of the age: and further, with the Bible as our guide, to anticipate that it will increase yet more.

The unrest existing today has about it two features that are worthy of notice:

(1) *It is practically universal in its extent.* Every country of note is afflicted with it, and most smaller countries as well. The civilization may be Eastern and ancient as in China, or Western and modern as in America and Britain: it matters not. The iron rule of Communism,

---

[2] *Scripture Truth*, Volume 40, 1959-1961, page 17

slaughtering millions of human beings to attain its purpose, may appear to have abolished it; but beneath the surface it exists; and in lands of greater freedom the wind of agitation and upheaval blows strongly. It may soon become a hurricane.

(2) *The unrest today is touching every department of human thought and activity.* It never did this before. Empires have risen and flourished and decayed, while repose has rested upon the world of philosophy and the applied sciences. Today violent changes are marked in all directions. Men's minds are working with almost superhuman energy in formulating new ideas and theories—social, political and theological—and in the manufacture of wonderful contrivances.

What does it all mean? That is the question which surely must be uppermost in the mind of every sober observer. For the Christian, who bows to the Word of God, and accepts the light it sheds, there is no difficulty in discovering the answer. Human histories give us at the best imperfect details of a few of the happenings of time; the Bible alone reveals to us the golden thread of Divine purpose, running through all history. Let us attempt to discern this by the guidance of the Holy Spirit of God, and so obtain the Divine answer.

Most of our readers are aware that before the Flood government did not exist. That age culminated in such violence and corruption that destruction was the only remedy—see Genesis 6:1-13.

On the cleansed earth government was instituted in the person of Noah—see Genesis 9:1-6. After the break-up of Babel, the authority seems to have departed from the main line of Noah's descendants, and each separate family began to range itself under its own tribal head, and the idea of kingship arose. There was no fresh development in regard to government on God's part until He called His people Israel out of Egypt, that He, the great Jehovah, might exercise authority in their midst.

The moment He chose for doing this was most significant. Egypt, almost the oldest of the nations, had risen to the highest point of her glory, having expelled the alien dynasty of 'Shepherd Kings', and become united under the rule of powerful and warlike native Pharaohs, who carried their conquests to the Euphrates. Then it was that God asserted His right to His people, and smote the oppressor a heavy blow, which evidently was the beginning of decline for that empire. He carried His people, in spite of their perverseness, into the land of promise. Jehovah claimed that land as His, taking possession of it by His people. He claimed it as His, in token that the whole earth is His. Twice is He spoken of as 'Lord of all the earth' in connection with the passage of the Jordan—see Joshua 3:11, 13.

Arrived in the land of promise, the people tired of being peculiar, in having God alone as their invisible Leader, and they clamoured for a visible human king. This, though a serious departure from God, was permitted and, after they had bitter experience of the man after their own hearts, God raised up David, the man after His own heart, placing him as a shepherd over His people, and extending his kingdom by crowning his arms with success. The diadem—which was indeed not that of Israel only, but of the whole world—was placed upon his brow and confirmed to his seed. For a brief time it was worn by him and by Solomon his successor.

Then came the inevitable story of decline. The kingdom was divided, only the smaller portion following the wearers of David's diadem; and they declined in power, as the departure, in spite of occasional, God-given revivals, became more and more pronounced.

At last the end came. Zedekiah, the last wearer of the diadem—though perhaps he wore it only in name—added treachery to his many sins, and dishonoured the name of his God. Whereupon, as recorded no less than three times in Scripture—2 Kings 25; 2 Chronicles 36; Jeremiah 52—Jerusalem fell before the Babylonians, and the dominion passed into the hands of Nebuchadnezzar. Thus 'the times of the Gentiles' set in.

Just at this time by the pen of the prophet Ezekiel remarkable words were written. As the diadem, which was, be it remembered, not of Israel only, but rather of the whole earth, fell from the brow of the last, apostate prince of David's line, struck thence by the hand of God in retributive judgment, these words were written. They are so important that we reproduce them in full.

> 'And thou, profane wicked prince of Israel, whose day is come, when iniquity shall have an end, Thus saith the Lord GOD: Remove the diadem, and take off the crown: this shall not be the same: exalt him that is low, and abase him that is high. I will overturn, overturn, overturn, it: and it shall be no more, until He come whose right it is; and I will give it Him' (Ezekiel 21:25-27).

How wonderfully illuminating! How revealing, the beam of light here thrown over the dark pages of human history since that day! The diadem has indeed been removed, and if a comprehensive history of the world could be compiled, it would prove to be but a record of the various efforts of men and nations to exalt themselves and seize upon the diadem, and of the sure and skilful way in which, when they appeared to have achieved their object, God has abased and overturned them.

A vision of this was granted to Daniel, which he has recorded in chapter 7 of his prophecy. It confirmed the dream previously given to Nebuchadnezzar, recorded in chapter 2. For a brief moment it seemed as if the diadem was to belong to that great king. But exalting himself above measure, he was painfully abased in abject madness, as recorded in chapter 4. Not long after, his great Babylon fell and was overturned. So too it was with the succeeding empires—Persian, Greek and Roman. Each ran its day, and each was overturned at the end.

Since the dissolution of the Roman Empire, no great empire, holding practically the civilized earth in its grip, has been permitted to arise. True, nearly a century ago men began to talk of a British Empire, for Queen Victoria had been proclaimed Empress of India. All that is passed however; and its dissolution—if an empire really did exist—proceeds steadily. Two great wars of world-wide dimensions have taken place; and today both Asia and Europe resemble armed camps. The diadem of the earth is lost; it is 'no more'. Powerful nations, that wish to regain it, hesitate; fearing lest in overturning others, they overturn themselves.

The present state of extremely unstable equilibrium cannot, however, go on for ever. Not a few are aware of this and talk vaguely of a coming 'Armageddon', meaning by this a great conflict which will embroil the whole civilized earth. They appear to forget that when this word is used in Revelation 16:13-16, what is predicted is not a frightful conflict of man against man, but rather the bold and impious hurling of the united forces of men against God. It is more than possible, however, that these warnings of coming ills do herald the near approach of the real Armageddon. Their words, like those of Caiaphas in John 11:49-52, may mean more than they themselves are conscious of.

New forces of great strength have arisen in these later years. In lands, where some form of Christianity still lingers, they centre themselves around the idea of 'the brotherhood of man' based on 'the universal fatherhood of God'. The new, progressive, humanistic theology, Unitarianism, Socialism, are all branches of this root idea. More imposing still is the atheistic Communism, which now dominates the minds and actions of great nations, containing about a third of the human race. All this in the hands of Satan may well prepare the way for the last great federation of mankind, to get ready for Antichrist.

Some may wish to observe that the Messiah, to whom the diadem really belongs, has already come. He has indeed: but not to assert those rights, but rather allowing man to have his hour, and the power of darkness to assert itself, that He might accomplish redemption by His death. Satan, who profanely has usurped the diadem, actually offered it to Him during the temptation in the wilderness. He refused it, and chose not that short and easy cut to glory, but the toilsome road that lay through death and resurrection— 'ought not Christ to have suffered these things, and to enter into His glory?' (Luke 24:26).

He did, however, plainly predict the coming of another prince, who would accept a diadem—purporting to be the true diadem of the earth—from the hands of Satan. 'I am come in My Father's name, and ye receive Me not: if another shall come in his own name, him ye will receive' (John 5:43).

In the days of the coming great trinity of evil—the dragon, the beast and the false prophet, of whom we read in Revelation 13—it will seem as if at last Ezekiel's prophecy was reversed and nullified. Men will have federated themselves into such a condition of so-called 'brotherhood', that it will only need the appearance of an unscrupulous 'superman', to seize the reins of power, and institute the most monstrous tyranny the world will ever witness. Let that state of things be reached, and what can save men from the net they have cast for their own feet? Yet a vast majority may even glory in the tyranny established. They will say, 'Peace and safety', thinking that at last the diadem is recovered so permanently, that no more overturnings need be feared.

But, 'when they shall say, Peace and safety; then sudden destruction cometh upon them' (1 Thessalonians 5:3). The last line of Ezekiel's prophecy will find sudden fulfilment. The last great overturning will take place in the true Armageddon. First, both the beast and false prophet and their armies will be destroyed by the sudden appearing of Him, 'whose right it is'. Shortly after, as we judge, the imposing northern powers, Gog, the prince of Rosh, Meshech, Tubal, and their many allies, will have the tremendous overthrow, predicted in Ezekiel 38 and 39. The last and decisive overturning will have taken place.

In that day the long-lost diadem, brilliant then, not only with the gems of creation, but with the brighter jewels of redemption, will be seen upon the head of the once rejected Man of Nazareth, our adorable Lord Jesus. Thence it will never be removed, for though at the end of the thousand years of His righteous reign there will be the rebellion engineered by a released Satan, as foretold in Revelation 20:7-10, this *uprising* will be instantly crushed, so that it never will become an *overturning*. Upon His sacred brow the diadem will have found its permanent, its eternal, resting-place.

In view of these things, what shall we say? Let us in the first place not be disturbed in mind, as we view the unrest and the spirit of upheaval which fills the earth today. Let us rather be concerned that we keep flying the flag of true testimony to Christ, and the Gospel which is centred in Him. God does not vary His plan of action as men invariably have to do. The instructions given by our Lord at the outset still stand good—the Holy Spirit has come and we follow the first disciples, as He said, 'ye shall be witnesses unto Me' (Acts 1:8).

Then further, let us not join hands with the world nor aid its schemes and movements, which, though they may not know it, are paving the way for Antichrist. Let us abide in communion with the Father and the Son, when our attitude towards the men of the world will be as the Scripture directs: we shall, as much as lies in us, 'live peaceably with all men', and instead of being overcome of evil, 'overcome evil with good' (Romans 12:18, 21).

Lastly, we shall treasure in our hearts the thought that all the unrest and overturning is only, 'until He come'. Shall we not turn our eyes toward the sun-rising of that long-looked for day, and say, 'Even so, come, Lord Jesus'?

Other Books by F. B. Hole
from Scripture Truth Publications

Isaiah
> ISBN 978-0-901860-72-9 (paperback)
> 192 pages; August 2013

Key Teachings
> ISBN 978-0-901860-16-3 (paperback)
> 151 pages; June 1998

Salvation
> ISBN 978-0-901860-17-0 (paperback)
> 212 pages; January 2015

"The Epistle of Christ" (editor)
> ISBN 978-0-901860-73-6 (paperback)
> 140 pages; March 2008

NEW TESTAMENT COMMENTARY SERIES:

The Gospels and Acts
> ISBN 978-0-901860-42-2 (paperback)
> ISBN 978-0-901860-46-0 (hardback)
> 392 pages; February 2007

Romans and Corinthians
> ISBN 978-0-901860-43-9 (paperback)
> ISBN 978-0-901860-47-7 (hardback)
> 176 pages; February 2007

Galatians to Philemon
> ISBN 978-0-901860-44-6 (paperback)
> ISBN 978-0-901860-48-4 (hardback)
> 204 pages; February 2007

Hebrews to Revelation
> ISBN 978-0-901860-45-3 (paperback)
> ISBN 978-0-901860-49-1 (hardback)
> 304 pages; February 2007

www.ingramcontent.com/pod-product-compliance
Lightning Source LLC
Chambersburg PA
CBHW072344090426
42741CB00012B/2910